# JANE GREY

## NINE DAYS
## QUEEN

## ALISON PLOWDEN

The
History
Press

This book was first published in 2003 by
Sutton Publishing

This paperback edition first published in 2004
Reprinted 2004, 2006

Reprinted in 2009 by
The History Press
The Mill, Brimscombe Port,
Stroud, Gloucestershire, GL5 2QG
www.thehistorypress.co.uk

British Library Cataloguing in Publication Data
A catalogue record for this book is available from the British
Library.

ISBN 978 0 7509 3769 6

Typeset in 11/13pt Photina.
Typesetting and origination by
Sutton Publishing Limited.
Printed and bound in Great Britain by Athenaeum Press Ltd.

# CONTENTS

# Chronology

# PROLOGUE

Today I saw Lady Jane Grey walking in a grand procession to the Tower. She is now called Queen, but is not popular, for the hearts of the people are with Mary, the Spanish Queen's daughter. This Jane is very short and thin, but prettily shaped and graceful. She has small features and a well-made nose, the mouth flexible and the lips red. The eyebrows are arched and darker than her hair, which is nearly red. Her eyes are sparkling and reddish brown in colour. I stood so near her grace that I noticed her colour was good but freckled. When she smiled she showed her teeth, which are white and sharp. In all a gracious and animated figure. She wore a dress of green velvet stamped with gold, with large sleeves. Her headdress was a white coif with many jewels. She walked under a canopy, her mother carrying her long train, and her husband Guildford walking by her, dressed all in white and gold, a very tall strong boy with light hair, who paid her much attention. The new Queen was mounted on very high chopines to make her look much taller, which were concealed by her robes, as she is very small and short. Many ladies followed, with noblemen, but this lady is very heretical and has never heard Mass, and some great people did not come into the procession for that reason.

Baptista Spinola, 10 July 1553

# ONE

## FOREBEARS

Eighth Henry ruling this land,
He had a sister fair . . .
And being come to England's Court,
She oft beheld a knight,
Charles Brandon nam'd, in whose fair eyes,
She chiefly took delight.
*Song of an English Knight* (The Suffolk Garland)

On a spring day in the year 1533 Henry Grey, marquess of Dorset, and the king's niece Lady Frances Brandon were married in the chapel at Suffolk Place, London, the home of the bride's parents. There is no reason to suppose that any romance was involved. Marriages at this level were, with very rare exceptions, strictly business arrangements, planned with financial and/or dynastic advantage in mind. In this case, however, the existence of a long-standing bond of friendship and shared experience between the Brandons and the Greys makes it likely that the young people concerned – Frances was not quite sixteen, Henry Grey about a year older – would have had more opportunity than many such couples of getting to know one another before the knot was tied.

At first glance it might have seemed a somewhat unequal match for the bride, with her impressive royal connections, but the Greys – their name is said to derive from the castle of Croy in Picardy – were an ancient and well-respected family with royal connections of their own. Recorded as being settled at Rotherfield in Oxfordshire shortly after the Conquest, their first mention in Dugdale's *Baronage* concerns Henry de Grey who received a grant of land at Thurrock in Essex from King Richard Lionheart in 1194 and, according to Dugdale, it was from the sons of this Henry that the numerous Greys of Wilton and Ruthyn were descended.[1] Edward, eldest son by a second marriage of the third Lord Grey of Ruthyn, married the heiress to the barony of Ferrers of Groby in Leicestershire and it was their son, Sir John Grey of Groby, who, in the middle of the fifteenth century, took to wife Elizabeth, the daughter of Richard Woodville of Grafton near Stony Stratford. This marriage was more or less contemporaneous with the early stages of that long-drawn-out, murderous family quarrel between York and Lancaster, conveniently known as the Wars of the Roses, and John Grey was killed fighting on the Lancastrian side at the second battle of St Albans in 1461. Three years later his widow, a beautiful but designing lady, so captivated the impressionable Yorkist king, Edward IV, that he married her – an unpopular misalliance widely held to have contributed to the eventual downfall of his house.

Elizabeth Woodville, as she is always better known, was notorious for the strength and tenacity of her family feelings, and she worked hard to promote the interests of her sons by her first marriage. Thomas, the elder, was created marquess of Dorset by his stepfather and looked to be all set for a secure and prosperous future. Then, suddenly, in April 1483 Edward IV was dead. By the end of the summer the throne had been seized by his brother Richard of Gloucester and his two young sons – 'the little princes in the Tower' – had disappeared from public view. That autumn there was an unsuccessful counter-coup led by Henry Stafford, duke of Buckingham, and supported by, among others, the Woodvilles and the Greys. The attempt to unseat King Richard collapsed and Buckingham was executed, but Thomas Grey and *his* young son escaped to Brittany where Henry Tudor, earl of Richmond, the last surviving male representative of the house of Lancaster, had been living in precarious exile for the past twelve years. Also among the select band of political refugees now gathering across the Channel were the brothers William and Thomas Brandon from East Anglia.

Unlike the Greys, the Brandons could not claim ancient or noble lineage, their immediate forebears having been small merchant traders based around the Norfolk port of Lynn. They were, however, on their way up. Their father, having made a good marriage and been fortunate in his business ventures, had invested in landed property, acquired a knighthood and set himself up as a prominent and 'worshipful' member of local society. The family had always been Yorkists loyal to Edward IV – William and Thomas had both been members of his household – but in 1483 they appear to have gambled on the overthrow of Richard Crookback and were consequently obliged to leave the country in a hurry.

That Christmas Henry Tudor made his celebrated solemn vow 'that so soon as he should be king he would marry Elizabeth, King Edward's daughter', after which his assembled followers did him homage 'as though he had been already created king'.[2] But the New Year was not a happy one for the Lancastrian/Tudor cause. Henry himself only narrowly avoided being handed over by his Breton hosts and was forced to make a dash for the frontier to seek the protection of the king of France – so perhaps it was hardly surprising that some members of his entourage should have begun to have second thoughts. The marquess of Dorset in particular had been receiving some very tempting offers from England, so that 'partly despairing for that cause of Earl Henry's success, partly suborned by King Richard's fair promises, [he] departed privily in the night time from Paris, and with great journeys travelled

3

into Flanders'.[3] This had serious implications for the exiles, as Dorset knew all their secrets, and he was pursued and 'persuaded' to return.

It was presumably this display of untrustworthiness that led to the marquess being left behind as one of the sureties for loans received from the French government when Henry Tudor finally set out to make his historic bid for the English throne. But the two Brandons were members of the little expeditionary force which sailed from Harfleur on 1 August 1485 and William Brandon, acting as Henry's standard-bearer, was to die a hero's death at Bosworth, struck down in the thick of the battle by King Richard himself.

Dorset was called home and became one of the new king Henry VII's councillors but suffered a brief eclipse at the time of the first Yorkist rising in 1487 when the king, remembering that worrying episode in France, ordered him to be placed in preventive detention in the Tower, although the order was accompanied by a fair message 'that he should bear that disgrace with patience, for that the king meant not his hurt' – his lordship was, after all, the new queen's half-brother. He was released after a few months with, it seems, no hard feelings on either side and two years later was given a command in Henry's only foreign war. Thomas Brandon, meanwhile, continued to serve the king as a councillor and increasingly on diplomatic missions abroad, but it was William's son – born, according to one authority, during his father's exile and christened Charles in honour of the king of France – who would be responsible for the family's rise to semi-royal grandeur.

Sponsored by his uncle, young Charles had begun his career at court in unspectacular fashion as a humble esquire of the body, and it was not until the accession of the second Henry Tudor in April 1509 that his fortunes took their dramatic upward turn. The new king of England was still a teenager and the nation, in particular the property-owning classes who had been finding the old king's regime increasingly oppressive and expensive, went wild with delight over their 'natural, young, lusty and courageous prince and sovereign lord King Harry the eighth'. The intelligentsia, too, were in transports over the appearance of this 'new and auspicious star', this charismatic Christian prince who spoke so earnestly about his love of learning, his respect for justice and virtue; while foreign observers almost ran out of adjectives in their efforts to describe his liberality, his magnificence, his amazing good looks, physical presence and personal charm.

Thanks to old Henry's statesmanship and prudent housekeeping, young Henry had succeeded unopposed to a secure and solvent throne – an advantage not enjoyed by an English monarch for very nearly a century – and throughout that first carefree summer the court was given over to a season of 'continual festival'. Revels, tilts and tournaments, pageants, banquets and 'disguises' followed one another in a non-stop, glittering, extravagant stream and conspicuous among the crowd of light-hearted, boisterous young men eager to help the king enjoy himself was Charles Brandon. It is probable that they were already friends, drawn together by a shared interest in sport, for Charles, like Henry, was a fine all-round athlete, tireless in the hunting field and a skilful and courageous performer in the jousts – that elaborate medieval war game so beloved by the English nobility. A cheerful, good-natured extrovert, without very much in the way of intellectual equipment, he made a perfect foil for his resplendent sovereign lord to whom he offered an uncritical, dog-like devotion. Henry found him excellent company and before long Charles was recognised as a leading member of the charmed circle of royal intimates.

The perquisites of this favoured position were well worth having, and Charles Brandon quickly became Marshal of the Household, Master of the Horse, Keeper of the important royal estate of Wanstead in Essex and Ranger of the New Forest. He was knighted, showered with stewardships, receiverships, wardships and valuable licences to export wool, leather, lead and tin – and it was pretty clear that this was only the beginning.

By the winter of 1512 the king was busy preparing for his first military adventure overseas. England had recently joined an offensive league of European powers aimed at containing French expansion in northern Italy and Henry was impatient to prove his manhood on the field of battle where, naturally, his best friend would fill a major supporting role. Everyone expected the king to confer a title on Brandon before they crossed the Channel, but as it happened his first step in rank came, ironically enough, via the Grey family in the person of his eight-year-old ward and affianced wife Elizabeth, daughter and heiress of the late John Grey, Viscount Lisle, and great-granddaughter of Edward Grey, Baron Ferrers of Groby.

By now in his late twenties, Charles Brandon already had quite a colourful matrimonial career behind him. Back in 1505 or thereabouts he had become engaged to Anne Browne, daughter of the Governor of Calais. The couple were betrothed *per verba de praesenti*, thus entering into a contract regarded as binding in canon law even if no church ceremony followed the exchange of vows. But it was not uncommon for an unprincipled man to repudiate his fiancée if someone better turned up, even if cohabitation had taken place, and this is what seems to have happened here. Certainly Charles and Anne had slept together without benefit of clergy, for she bore him a daughter some time in 1506. The faithless Charles, meanwhile, had married Margaret Mortimer, a wealthy widow approximately twice his age, prompting a Venetian observer of the English social scene to comment caustically on the mercenary habits of young men who were willing to marry for money ladies old enough to be their mothers. This union, though, was short-lived, being annulled, possibly as a result of action by the Browne family, on the grounds of the groom's pre-contract and cohabitation with his previous partner. Charles and Anne then went through a public marriage ceremony and another daughter was born in the summer of 1510. Anne Browne died shortly afterwards and in December 1512 her widower acquired the wardship of Elizabeth Grey.[4]

Under English law the wardship of any minor child who inherited landed property passed automatically to the Crown, which normally gave (or, more usually, sold) it back to the relatives of the child concerned or some other favoured applicant. The guardian was then free to enjoy the income from the property until the minor came of age – by which time he would either have sold his ward's marriage to the highest bidder or else have arranged a marriage ensuring that control of the inheritance remained within his own family circle, so no one was surprised when, in the spring of 1513, Charles Brandon announced his engagement to Elizabeth Grey. On 15 May Letters Patent were issued creating him Viscount Lisle in right of his 'wife' and a few weeks later the new Lord Lisle accompanied the king to France as 'marshal of the host and captain of the fore-ward' with three thousand men under his command.

The rest of the summer was spent playing soldiers in Picardy, where both Henry and Viscount Lisle duly established their reputations as fighting men and the king astonished everyone by his courage and endurance in the face of the enemy. It is true that the enemy proved disappointingly elusive and it was bad luck that Henry should have missed the best bit of action – a scrambling cavalry skirmish near Guinegate, later dignified with the title of the Battle of the Spurs. But on the whole it was a very nice little war and Henry, firing a cannon with his own hands, dubbing knights on the field of battle and riding round the camp at night in full armour, enjoyed himself so much that he quite failed to notice that the two frontier towns of Therouanne and Tournai, captured by the English army, were of value only to his ally, the Hapsburg Emperor Maximilian.

Autumn found both the friends at Lille in southern Flanders as guests at the court of Margaret of Austria, Regent of the Netherlands, and, encouraged by the king, Lord Lisle embarked on a playful flirtation with his hostess. Unfortunately, what had begun as a bit of a joke became the subject of gossip and rumours of an impending marriage had to be hurriedly denied by embarrassed diplomats. Lord Lisle might be an important figure at the English court – he and the king's almoner, a rising cleric named Thomas Wolsey, were said to govern everything between them – but by no stretch of the imagination could he be regarded as husband material for a Hapsburg princess accustomed to being wooed by reigning monarchs.

All the same Charles Brandon was about to take a giant step up the social ladder when, on 1 February, he was created duke of Suffolk, a title previously held by the great Yorkist family of de la Pole. This sudden and startling elevation of the king's favourite – there were currently only two other dukes in England – raised eyebrows and hackles in establishment circles. 'Many people considered it very surprising that Charles should be so honoured' observed the contemporary historian Polydore Vergil. There were, of course, some quite sound political reasons for the move. Apart from sending an unmistakable message to Richard de la Pole, the last significant Yorkist claimant still at large on the Continent, the new duke, allied with Wolsey, would help to counter the influence of the powerful Howard family and their faction at the council table. But there seems no reason to doubt that Henry was also motivated by a genuine affection for his 'dearest Brandon' and a desire to reward and encourage him.

If 1514 marked a decisive stage in the saga of the Brandon family, it was also notable for an abrupt change of direction in English foreign policy. The king had fallen out with his European allies, having belatedly realised the extent to which they had been making use of him for their own ends, and that summer he concluded an alliance with France to be sealed by the marriage of his sister Mary to the French king, Louis XII.

Nineteen-year-old Mary Tudor, the youngest surviving child of Henry VII and Elizabeth of York, was the beauty of the English royal family – with her elegant figure, perfect complexion and wonderful red-gold hair, she was generally conceded to have been one of the loveliest women of her day. High-spirited, wilful and more than a little spoilt, in the five years since her father's death she had been enjoying a most unusual amount of fun and freedom for an unmarried princess; but the king was fond of his sister, who shared his exuberant delight in dancing, party-going, dressing up and showing off, and he liked having her around and encouraged her to play a full part in the hectic social life of the court. The dangers inherent in this sort of permissiveness were obvious enough – it was not for nothing that royal brides were normally shipped off to their husbands the moment they became nubile. Mary was a warm-blooded young woman surrounded by the pick of the eligible men in the kingdom, and inevitably she had formed an attachment of her own, the object of her affections being no less a person than the controversial new duke of Suffolk. She would, of course, have known him from a distance since childhood, but by 1514 what may perhaps have begun as a little girl's hero-worship for one of her brother's lordly friends had ripened into something altogether more mature.

There was no scandal. No gossip linking the princess's name with the duke had yet reached the outside world, but within the family the affair seems to have been a pretty open secret. Mary herself had confided in her brother, telling him that she loved Charles Brandon and would only agree to marry the king of France – a widower in his fifties and a martyr to gout – on condition that, as soon as she was free again, Henry would allow her to make her own choice as her own heart and mind should be best pleased.

9

'And upon that your great comfort and faithful promise', she wrote later, 'I assented to the said marriage; else I would never have granted to, as at the same time I showed unto you more at large.'[5]

On this understanding, it seems, the bargain was struck and Mary sailed from Dover at the beginning of October, slightly cheered by the magnificence of her trousseau. Her beauty and charm made an excellent impression on the French, and at her first meeting with Louis he threw his arms round her neck and 'kissed her as kindly as if he had been five-and-twenty'. Not surprisingly such an ill-assorted couple were made the butt of unkind jokes in some quarters – in Spain it was being predicted that his young wife would soon be the death of a bridegroom in his dotage. To the outward eye, however, Louis appeared very jovial and in love. He had temporarily quite thrown off his invalidish habits, boasting that on his wedding night he had 'crossed the river' three times and would have done more had he chosen. Apart from a brief unpleasantness over the dismissal of some of Mary's English attendants, he proved an indulgent and generous husband and by the time Charles Brandon paid a visit to France in November the newly-weds had established quite a cosy relationship.

Suffolk had come over with Thomas Grey, 2nd marquess of Dorset, who had succeeded his father back in 1501. A military man and another notable performer in the jousts, he and the duke were to take part in a tournament celebrating Mary's forthcoming coronation, but Suffolk had also been entrusted with certain confidential matters to be discussed with the French in private. He had an audience with the king and queen at Beauvais, where he found Louis lying on a couch with Mary sitting beside him, and was able to report 'that never queen behaved herself more wisely and honourably, and so say all the noblemen of France'.[6] Charles Brandon was clearly impressed by her dignity and restraint which, he told Henry, 'rejoiced me not a little', adding significantly, 'your grace knows why'. It sounds rather as if he had been afraid Mary might embarrass him in public, but he need not have worried. The queen of France knew what was due to her position and she received her brother's envoy with perfect sangfroid.

Mary's marriage to King Louis lasted for just eighty-two days and when he collapsed and died on New Year's Eve 1514 her situation changed abruptly. Much to her dismay, she found herself obliged to endure the forty days of strict seclusion imposed by French custom – a period of mourning or, more accurately, quarantine, designed to ensure that if a widowed queen proved to be pregnant, there should be as little doubt as possible as to the paternity of her child. Mary's protests that to the best of her knowledge she was *not* pregnant were disregarded, and she was bundled off to the Hotel de Cluny to spend six weeks behind drawn curtains in a stuffy, black-draped mourning chamber. Here, cut off from the outside world, she began to panic in case Henry might already be planning another foreign match for her while she was helpless to stop him. Terror that he meant to break his word is apparent in every line of a letter written from Cluny in January:

Sir, I beseech your grace that you will keep all the promises that you promised me when I took my leave of you by the waterside. Sir, your grace knoweth well that I did marry for your pleasure at this time and now I trust you will suffer me to marry as me liketh for to do . . . wherefore I beseech your grace for to be a good lord and brother unto me.[7]

Exactly what the king was planning for his sister's future remains a trifle unclear. If he did *not* intend to honour his famous promises of the previous autumn, it was perhaps not very wise to appoint the duke of Suffolk as head of the mission charged with the task of winding up her affairs in

France. But Henry trusted his friend. He had no reason not to do so. Charles Brandon was, after all, his own creation, dependent on royal favour and bounty for his very existence. He did, however, take the precaution of asking the duke for a solemn undertaking that he would keep his relations with Mary on a strictly formal basis while they were abroad. There may quite possibly have been some kind of understanding that if he succeeded in extricating the queen dowager on satisfactory financial terms, the king would be prepared to give them his blessing – rumours of a marriage were already going round – but Suffolk was probably less concerned just then with thoughts of romance than with the daunting prospect of having to drive a bargain with the French over Mary's plate and jewels and dower rights. He was, therefore, seriously taken aback when he arrived in France at the end of January to discover that the new king, Louis's big foxy-faced cousin François d'Angoulême, apparently knew all about his personal affairs.

Brandon's first interview with Mary was even more unnerving. As soon as they were alone together the distracted widow proceeded to unloose on him all the pent-up emotion of the past few weeks. The more she thought about it the more convinced she had become that his mission was a trap to lure her back to England to be forced into another loveless political alliance and she would rather be torn in pieces – either that, or his enemies on the council would find some way of preventing their marriage. Nothing her harassed sweetheart could say would pacify her, and in floods of tears – according to the duke he had never seen a woman so weep – she presented him with an ultimatum: either he agreed to marry her there and then, while they had the chance, or he 'might never look to have the same proffer again'. With his promise to Henry weighing heavily on his conscience, Suffolk tried to evade the issue (or so he said later) but his protests were swept aside. Mary reminded him that she had her brother's promise that next time she might marry as she pleased and they might never have such an opportunity again. She would almost certainly have added that he couldn't really love her if he was not willing to take so small a risk for her sake.

All this put Charles Brandon in an appalling quandary. His whole career had been founded on his commitment to the Tudor family and now he was fairly and squarely caught between the Scylla and Charybdis of Tudor passion and Tudor despotism. He was genuinely devoted to his sovereign lord and stood in very healthy awe of him, but it is hard for any man to stand like a stone while the loveliest princess in Europe is literally begging and praying him to take her to his bed. And there was something else. Although it was not tactful to draw attention to it, the fact remained that after nearly six years of marriage Henry's Spanish wife Catherine of Aragon had not yet given him a living heir. It was by no means impossible that his younger sister might found a new royal line and visions of fathering a future king of England must surely have passed through Suffolk's head – for all his bluff, easy-going exterior he was an ambitious man. Forced into the unaccustomed exercise of thinking on his feet, Mary's tears and intimations of dynastic immortality overcame considerations of trust and honour, self-restraint, even of self-preservation, and on an undisclosed date in February 1515 Charles Brandon and Mary Tudor, queen of France, were married very quietly indeed in the chapel at Cluny, with only a handful of the bride's personal servants as witnesses.

Confession could not long be postponed. By the beginning of March reports of that furtive ceremony at Cluny were circulating freely in Paris and on the 5th of the month Charles Brandon sat down to write a difficult letter to his friend Thomas Wolsey, now archbishop of York, explaining that 'the queen would never let me be in rest till I had granted her to be married. And so, to be plain with you, I have married her heartily, and have lyen with her, insomuch that I fear me lest she be with child. My lord,' he went on, 'I am not in a little sorrow lest the king should know of it and be displeased with me, for I assure you I had rather have died than he should be miscontent.' He ended by begging for Wolsey's 'especial help' in breaking the news to Henry, for 'I have as heavy a heart as any man living and shall have till I may hear good tidings from you.'[8]

There followed a fortnight's painful suspense and Wolsey's reply when it came was not encouraging. The king's first reaction had been one of utter disbelief that the man he had loved and trusted best could have so wantonly betrayed his confidence. Wolsey had had to show him Suffolk's letter before he would give it credence and now he was bitterly hurt and angry. 'Cursed be the blind affection and counsel that hath brought you hereunto,' wrote the archbishop grimly, 'fearing that such sudden and unadvised dealing shall have sudden repentance.' Let Charles Brandon make no mistake, by his acts and doings he had put himself 'in the greatest danger that ever man was in'.[9]

Shaking in their shoes, the culprits now hastened to throw themselves on the king's mercy, acknowledging their fault and beseeching forgiveness. 'Sir, for the passion of God', cried the duke, 'let it not be in your heart against me, and rather than you should hold me in mistrust, strike off my head and let me not live.'[10] For her part, Mary did her best to take the blame on herself. She knew she had constrained my lord of Suffolk to break his promise, but it was only because she had been thrown into such terrible 'consternation, fear and doubt' that their marriage might somehow be prevented. She, too, begged for forgiveness, 'and that it will please your grace to write to me and to my lord of Suffolk some comfortable words'.[11]

No such words were forthcoming, but all the same it was soon obvious from Wolsey's letters that Henry's wrath could be assuaged at a price – and a heavy financial penalty was imposed on the lovers, who were ordered to repay all the costs of Mary's first marriage – her dowry, her trousseau and her wedding journey. Suffolk also had to surrender his wardship of Elizabeth Grey (he had broken off his engagement to her some time in the previous year) but he was allowed to keep his other offices and estates.

It was the beginning of May before Mary and her new husband were finally free to return to England and they had a grand wedding at Greenwich on the 13th in the presence of the whole court, apparently fully restored to royal favour. The Venetian ambassador was amazed and hesitated to offer congratulations until he was quite sure they would be acceptable. But in spite of all the accounts of his dire displeasure relayed by Thomas Wolsey, it is pretty clear that the king had never intended to proceed to extremes against his best friend and his favourite sister. It is true that some of the older, more conservative members of the Privy Council disapproved of the marriage, but Suffolk's genial good fellowship and athletic prowess made him a popular figure and, apart from his political rivals, few people seriously grudged him his good fortune. Few people, after all, could resist a romance, especially one with a happy ending – a rare enough event in royal circles. No one denied that it was an unequal match, but the general feeling on this aspect of Mary Tudor's love story was neatly summed up in the quatrain which appears beneath the portrait of the happy pair painted at about the time of their marriage and said to have been composed by the bridegroom himself:

> Cloth of gold, do not despise,
> Though thou be match'd with cloth of frieze.
> Cloth of frieze, be not too bold,
> Though thou be match'd with cloth of gold.

In February 1516, after a long history of miscarriages, babies stillborn or living only a few weeks, Queen Catherine of Aragon finally gave birth to a healthy child – a girl, christened Mary. The king was apparently delighted, saying to an ambassador who ventured to commiserate with him over the baby's sex that 'if it was a daughter this time, by God's grace the sons will follow'. A month later the Suffolks' first child was born – a boy, christened, naturally, Henry. The king's daughter survived, but his nephew did not, dying some time before his fifth birthday. The duchess of Suffolk (or the French queen, as she continued to be styled by everyone, including herself) went on to produce two daughters – Frances, born on St Francis's Day, 16 July 1517, and Eleanor two years later – then, in 1522, another son, also christened Henry. But there was still no prince of Wales and it was clear by this time that the queen would have no more children. All the same it was another five years before Henry first applied to Rome for a divorce or, more accurately, an annulment of his marriage, convinced, so he said, that he and Catherine were living in incestuous adultery and that was why God, whom he always regarded very much in the light of a senior partner, was refusing to give him sons. Quite a number of his subjects were equally convinced that the king's famous scruple of conscience had more to do with his infatuation for one of his wife's maids of honour, the fascinating brunette Anne Boleyn, than with any very pressing anxiety over the succession.

The divorce, or the king's Great Matter as it became known, was to dominate the English political scene for the best part of a decade and its ramifications would destroy the lives of many good men and women (Thomas Wolsey, cardinal archbishop, was one of its first casualties), but the Grey and Brandon families were not at first directly affected. Thomas Grey and Charles Brandon were both, of course, committed king's men, although the Suffolks were believed privately to disapprove of his proceedings and the French queen in particular was known to sympathise with her unfortunate sister-in-law. But by 1527 the Suffolks were themselves beginning to worry in case the legality of their own marriage might be called into question. The duke's erstwhile ward and fiancée, Elizabeth Grey, had died in 1519 but Dame Margaret Mortimer, the same who had once lived briefly as Brandon's wife, although a very old lady was still alive, and if now the legitimacy of the king's daughter and heir presumptive were to be challenged, the status of the Suffolk children would become a matter of considerable constitutional and personal importance.

The duke therefore consulted canon lawyers, who applied to Rome for a ruling on the matter and in May 1528 received the answer they wanted – a papal bull ratifying the original sentence of the archdeacon of London's court given in 1507 annulling the Brandon–Mortimer marriage. Margaret Mortimer died about this time, thus helpfully tidying up any loose ends; all the same in August 1529 the Suffolks took the additional precaution of having the new decree notorially attested before the bishop of Norwich and a posse of official witnesses.

The anxious parents could now begin to look round more confidently for husbands for their daughters. Their first choice for Frances was the duke of Norfolk's son Henry, earl of Surrey, but the Howards turned down the match because, it seemed, the dowry offered was too small. Then, in October 1530, Charles Brandon's old friend and comrade in arms Thomas Grey, marquess of Dorset, died, to be succeeded by his fourteen-year-old son Henry. The earl of Arundel was in the bidding for the wardship of the young marquess with a view to marrying him off to his daughter, Lady Katherine FitzAlan; but for reasons not disclosed, the young marquess chose to reject Lady Katherine and consequently Arundel withdrew from the competition. This opened up a window of opportunity for the duke of Suffolk and, with the king's approval, he stepped in to acquire the wardship for himself and with it a husband for *his* daughter.[12] Frances's future was thus honourably secured and her wedding, marking the union of two of England's leading families, was a suitably grand affair.

It also marked the last public appearance of Mary Tudor, the French queen. Mary had been very little at court during recent years, preferring to spend most of her time at Westhorpe Hall, the Suffolks' principal country seat in East Anglia, some 12 miles from Bury St Edmunds. Her absence seems to have been partly due to a natural reluctance to yield precedence to Mistress Anne Boleyn, and partly to her increasingly poor health. So as soon as the wedding festivities were over, she travelled back to Westhorpe alone with her younger daughter. Her husband was too busy running the king's errands to go with her and, although he paid a brief visit to his ailing wife some time early in May, he does not seem to have been with her when she slipped quietly away between seven and eight o'clock on the morning of 25 June. She was thirty-eight years old and the exact nature of her long wasting illness, of which the only recorded symptom was a pain in the side, is not known. It may have been cancer or, perhaps more likely in view of the Tudor family's medical history, tuberculosis.

In normal circumstances the wedding of the king's niece and the death of his sister might have attracted rather more public notice, but everyone's attention just then was focused on the unfolding drama of his majesty's own domestic problems, for in the spring of 1533 the bitter six-year battle for the divorce was reaching its climax. In spite of the fact that Queen Catherine was still stubbornly refusing to accept her relegation and that still no ruling had come from Rome, it was an open secret – in court circles at least – that Henry and his lady had been married in a very private ceremony at the end of January, and most people now knew that Anne Boleyn was pregnant. No one, therefore, was surprised when, late in May, Thomas Cranmer, the newly enthroned Archbishop of Canterbury, pronounced the king's first marriage to be null and void and his second good and lawful. Preparations were already well advanced for Queen Anne's coronation, scheduled to take place on 1 June, with the duke of Suffolk acting as High Constable for the occasion and as Steward for the feast that would follow. Small wonder then that he had been able to spare so little time for visiting Westhorpe.

As was customary, Charles Brandon did not attend his wife's funeral but every detail of the ritual pomp and ceremony due to her exalted station was meticulously observed. The coffin lay in state at Westhorpe for nearly a month before being removed to the abbey of St Edmundsbury for committal. At the head of the cortège walked a hundred poor men in black hoods and gowns and carrying wax tapers. Then came the domestic chaplains with the Westhorpe chapel cross, escorted by a contingent of barons, knights and gentlemen and followed by the officers of the household, Garter and Clarenceux Kings of Arms, and a representative from the French College of Heralds, all mounted on horses trapped to the ground with black. The hearse, or funeral car, was drawn by six horses and draped in black velvet with the late queen's motto, *La volonté de Dieu me suffit*, worked in fine gold, while over it was a rich canopy borne by four mounted knights. On the coffin itself lay an effigy of Mary arrayed in the state robes, the crown and panoply of a queen of France, while on either side hung banners painted with the proud escutcheons of her arms as a princess of England and queen dowager of France. Immediately behind the hearse and leading the family mourners rode Frances Grey, marchioness of Dorset, supported by her new husband and her eleven-year-old brother Henry, earl of Lincoln. There followed a cavalcade of noble ladies, each attended by a running footman, two mourning wagons or coaches and, bringing up the rear, the waiting women, yeomen and lesser servants on foot.

The 'right high and excellent princess and right Christian Queen Mary, late French Queen' was laid to rest in the great abbey church at Bury St Edmunds on 22 July and a handsome alabaster monument was presently erected over her tomb. Both abbey and monument were to be destroyed during the period of the dissolution of the monasteries, when so much else of the world Mary had known dissolved into rubble and firewood and shards of broken glass, but her coffin was saved and re-interred in the nearby church of St Mary. In 1784, when it was moved to a new resting place in the north-east corner of the chancel, the coffin was opened and the embalmed corpse was found to be in an amazingly good state of preservation. The teeth were complete and undecayed and the hair, almost two feet in length, had retained its red-gold colour – so much so that ghoulish souvenir hunters hurried to cut tresses from it.[13]

Mary Tudor, queen and duchess, had never been more than a minor figure on the historical stage and nothing in her life had affected the mainstream of great events. All she had ever asked for herself was a measure of personal happiness, and in that respect she had been more fortunate than most women in her position and century. Certainly the girl who had defiantly insisted on her right to be allowed to marry the man she loved never seems to have regretted it, and she can scarcely be blamed for failing to foresee the deadly inheritance, compounded of her own royal blood and her brother's capricious favouritism, which she had created for her innocent posterity.

The year 1533 continued to be an eventful one for both the Tudor and Brandon families. Barely two months after Mary's death Charles Brandon had married again. Rapid remarriage by both sexes was not unusual, but the fact that the duke of Suffolk's latest bride was the same age as his younger daughter – fourteen to his forty-eight or nine – and was already promised to his son gave the affair enough 'novelty', as one observer put it, to attract the attention of some political commentators.

Suffolk's fourth wife was another of his wards, the daughter and heiress of Lord Willoughby of Eresby, an important landowner in Suffolk and Lincolnshire. The duke had invested some £2,500 in the wardship of young Catherine Willoughby, who had been living under his roof for the past five years or so, being educated with his own daughters. She was a good-looking girl, healthy, intelligent and high-spirited, and he may very likely have been fond of her, but his motive for marrying her was pretty certainly a financial one. Frances's wedding had cost him over sixteen hundred pounds and Eleanor's was still to come, while Mary's outstanding debts to the Crown were yet to be finally settled. In the circumstances a rich wife (and the gossipy author of *The Spanish Chronicle* heard that the duchess of Suffolk, a baroness in her own right, was worth 15,000 ducats a year) would obviously be desirable. Young Catherine was conveniently ready to hand and the duke saw no reason to waste her on his son, who could be matched elsewhere easily enough. As it happened, Henry Brandon died the following spring, leaving the gossip-mongers to insinuate that his untimely end was due to grief at having been so heartlessly deprived of his fiancée.

Suffolk appears to have survived this second bereavement with tolerable equanimity and his new marriage was proving a success, the duchess providing him with two healthy sons in the space of two years. The king's domestic affairs, however, continued to be worryingly unsatisfactory. Henry had made powerful enemies both at home and abroad, and had ruthlessly manipulated the accepted laws of God and man in his determination to ensure that Anne Boleyn's child – the child which, he had convinced himself, would surely be a son – was born in wedlock, and all he had got for his pains was another useless girl. The birth of Elizabeth Tudor in September 1533 was a black disappointment for both her parents, but a good face had to be put on it before the world. A solemn *Te Deum* for the queen's safe delivery was sung in St Paul's in the presence of the city dignitaries and the new princess was given a suitably grand christening in the Friars Church at

Greenwich. The following spring parliament at Westminster passed an act making it a treasonable offence to question the validity of the king's divorce and second marriage and settling the succession on the lawfully begotten children of his 'most dear and entirely beloved wife Queen Anne', while Mary, his elder daughter and ex-heiress presumptive, was in future to be regarded 'but as a bastard'. Almost simultaneously the Pope in full consistory at Rome finally gave judgement on the matter of the royal divorce, pronouncing the marriage between Henry and Catherine of Aragon to have been good and lawful from the beginning.

The Brandon and Grey families had continued publicly to support the king throughout his various marital difficulties – Suffolk had been present at Elizabeth's christening and the dowager marchioness of Dorset officiated as one of the godmothers. The young Dorsets meanwhile were beginning their married life, dividing their time between London and the court and the family estates in Leicestershire. The 2nd marquess had begun to build a fine new mansion at Bradgate Park, three miles north-west of Leicester and about a mile and a half from the village of Groby on the edge of Charnwood Forest. The house, which was completed by his son, was a large, low, red-brick building, in the form of a square, decorated with turrets and an imposing gatehouse, and surrounded by a park six miles in circumference. John Leland, who visited Bradgate in the 1540s, remarked on its good and vigorous water supply and the well-wooded country round about; but for the Dorsets, who like most of their contemporaries were passionately addicted to field sports, its principal attraction was doubtless the abundance of game available on their doorstep.

Unlike his father and grandfather, the 3rd marquess showed no inclination for a career in soldiering or public affairs, and this was perhaps just as well, for in the 1530s public affairs were a more than usually dangerous pursuit. The parliament of 1534 had enacted a programme of revolutionary change codifying the English Church's breach with Rome and effectively privatising its enormous wealth, and in the spring of 1535 the king had officially assumed the title of Supreme Head of the Church of England with power to 'reform and redress all errors, heresies and abuses in the same'. It now became high treason 'maliciously' to deny this startling addition to the royal style and that summer Sir Thomas More and John Fisher, bishop of Rochester, paid the price of refusing to recognise Henry Tudor as their supreme earthly authority on matters spiritual.

In 1536 Queen Anne Boleyn was tried on charges of committing adultery with 'divers of the king's familiar servants', of incest with her brother George, of despising her marriage and 'imagining' the king's death. The trial was, of course, a mere formality and Anne was duly convicted of treason and beheaded on Tower Green on 19 May. Not content with killing the woman who had once been his great love, Henry had insisted on obtaining a decree of nullity and Thomas Cranmer obediently pronounced their union to have been invalid from the start, thus bastardising and disinheriting the two-year-old Elizabeth in her turn.

Within a matter of weeks the king had taken his third wife. A widower twice over – Catherine of Aragon having died at the beginning of the year – this marriage would be indisputably legal and Henry had every hope that the demurely respectable Jane Seymour, who came herself from a large family, would soon provide him with the male heir now so urgently needed. A second Act of Succession was passed in June ratifying the annulment of the Boleyn marriage and officially declaring Anne's daughter illegitimate. The succession was therefore to be vested in the issue of the king's third marriage but, just in case such issue were not forthcoming, it was enacted that Henry should be given the power to appoint an heir by will or letters patent – an extraordinary provision which indicates how acute the problem was becoming.

The marquess of Dorset was not having much luck in begetting a male heir either. Frances had given birth to a son and a daughter who both died in infancy but in 1537 she was pregnant again and another daughter was born who seemed likely to survive. The actual date of Jane Grey's birth is not recorded, although the month is said to have been October, but interest in the arrival of Lord and Lady Dorset's daughter was naturally eclipsed by the excitement over the birth at Hampton Court in the early hours of 12 October of a son to the king and Queen Jane Seymour. *Te Deums* were sung in St Paul's and every parish church in the city. Bells pealed, 2,000 rounds were fired from the Tower guns, bonfires blazed and everyone shut up shop and came out to celebrate. Impromptu street parties were organised as bands of musicians went about playing and singing loyal ballads in honour of the occasion and the prince's health was drunk in the free wine and beer which flowed in profusion from the conduits and from hogsheads provided by the civic authorities and by other prominent citizens. All that day, through the night and well into the next day the capital rocked and clashed in a great crescendo of relief and thanksgiving that at long last England had a prince of Wales. Messengers were dispatched to 'all the estates and cities of the realm' to spread the glad tidings and the whole country became almost hysterical with joy. As Bishop Latimer wrote to Thomas Cromwell from his Worcester diocese: 'Here is no less rejoicing in these parts from the birth of our prince, whom we hungered for so long, than there was, I trow, at the birth of John the Baptist . . . God give us grace to be thankful.'

The christening of England's Treasure, 'Prince Edward that goodly flower', took place three days after his birth in the chapel at Hampton Court amid scenes of suitable splendour. The dukes of Norfolk and Suffolk and Archbishop Thomas Cranmer were godfathers, the Lady Mary, godmother. The baby's other sister was also present, bearing the 'richly garnished' chrysom, or christening robe. This burden proved rather too much for the four-year-old Elizabeth, so 'the same lady for her tender age' was carried in the procession by Queen Jane's elder brother. The Grey family, however, was not represented. Old Lady Dorset had been appointed to carry the prince to his christening, but had been obliged to send her excuses because of sickness in the neighbourhood of her house at Croydon; and Frances Dorset was presumably still lying-in up at Bradgate with her husband in attendance. Their new daughter had been named in honour of the queen but she, poor soul, did not live to appreciate the compliment. A few days after Edward's christening she became so ill that the last sacraments were administered. She rallied briefly but by 24 October she was dead, killed most probably by puerperal sepsis, the scourge of all women in childbed. She was given a state funeral at Windsor, with the Princess Mary officiating as chief mourner and this time both Dorsets were present, the Lady Frances, as she was still generally known, riding in a chariot with other noble ladies. As it turned out, Jane Seymour was the only one of Henry's wives to be buried as queen and perhaps that was fair – she was, after all, the only one who had truly fulfilled her side of the bargain.

Jane had been buried and her son and her namesake baptised according to the familiar rites of the Catholic Church, but both these children were born on the cusp of that great social and spiritual upheaval known to history as the English Reformation, which was destined profoundly to affect the course not only of their lives but those of every other man, woman and child in the country. To say that had the Pope not been so disobliging over the matter of the king's divorce from his first wife there would have been no break with Rome is greatly to over-simplify the situation, but although Henry may not have intended to start a revolution that, in effect, is what he had done. There was in England a long tradition of anti-clerical feeling and smouldering religious radicalism going back to John Wyclif and the Lollards of the late fourteenth and early fifteenth centuries, which in the 1520s had received fresh impetus from Lutheran doctrines coming in from Germany, so that the king's Great Matter and the consequent schism served as the catalyst for a chain reaction that was to prove unexpectedly difficult to control. It is sometimes said that Henry's church remained Catholic without the Pope, but that is another over-simplification.

Changes *were* made, and some new ideas considered and experimented with. In 1537 the first English Bible, the so-called Matthew Bible, went on sale, followed in the spring of 1539 by the better known Great Bible, based on the translations of Tyndale and Coverdale. This quickly became a best-seller, running through six further editions in the next two years, and its effect on an increasingly literate and sophisticated public was electric. To the average concerned and educated citizen it meant that he and, for that matter, she were now, for the first time, in a position freely to study and interpret the word of God for themselves, which led in turn to the exhilarating realisation that it was possible for an individual to hold direct communion with God without having to depend on a priest to act as intermediary; and a conviction was growing among thoughtful men and women that priests could offer no scriptural authority for their claim to be the only channel through which the laity could hope to receive divine grace.

These revolutionary ideas took time to penetrate rural Leicestershire where little Jane Grey and her younger sister Katherine, born in 1539, were receiving the early training proper for children of their rank. Life at Bradgate when the family was in residence was lived on a grand scale. When Lord and Lady Dorset dined in public the Great Hall could accommodate some 200 persons and the meal would be served with almost as much ceremonial as that observed at court – each course being brought in to a flourish of trumpets. Foreign tourists were always amazed at the amount of food and drink the English seemed able to put away. 'They eat very frequently, at times more than is suitable,' remarked an Italian visitor, 'and are particularly fond of young swans, rabbits, deer and sea birds. They often eat mutton and beef, which is generally considered to be better here than anywhere else in the world.'[14] Nursery fare, however, would not have included the rich treats available to the grown-ups and consisted mainly of broths, jellies, custards, omelettes and other so-called 'white meats'. Nor would the little girls have had much share in their parents' social life. They do not seem to have accompanied their mother when she paid her ceremonial visits to the town of Leicester, where she would be received as befitted her status. There are entries in the town books recording the expenditure of 2s 6d by the mayoress and her sisters 'for strawberries and wine for my lady's grace'. On another occasion 4s was paid for 'a gallon of Ippocras, that was given to my lady's grace by mistress mayoress and her sisters, the wives of the aldermen of Leicester, who gave besides wafers, apples, pears and walnuts at the same time'.[15]

Although the Dorsets were regarded as princes by their neighbours, and certainly expected to be treated as such, little or nothing is known about their daughters' early years, which must be assumed to have followed the usual pattern for young noblewomen. The Ladies Jane and Katherine would have learned all the basics of good manners, and the feminine virtues of docility, passivity and obedience would have been inculcated at a very early age. When encountering their parents they would be expected to kneel and ask a blessing, and their parents' word was law. In the opinion of Luis Vives, the Spanish scholar invited by Catherine of Aragon to draw up a plan of studies for the Princess Mary, it was vitally important that a young girl's upbringing should be 'pure and chaste'. As soon as she was able to talk and run about, her companions should be other girls of her own age, and they should be supervised either by mother or nurse who could rule their play and pastimes and 'set them to honesty and virtue'. A young girl, too, must be allowed no opportunity to learn any 'uncleanly words, or wanton, or uncomely gesture when she is yet ignorant what she doth, and innocent' lest she should do the same when she was grown bigger and of more discretion; and parents must be careful never to allow any 'uncomely deed' to pass uncorrected, for it was in these first years that a child's character was formed.[16]

Lady Jane's formal education would most probably have begun about the age of four or five. It is possible that she would have learnt her alphabet – from letters printed on a horn book, a sheet of paper mounted on a wooden tablet and protected by a thin sheet of transparent horn – from her nurse Mrs Ellen, or from one of the waiting gentlewomen in the household. She may even have been taught to read by one of these ladies. Latin and religious instruction would have been the responsibility of Dr Harding, the domestic chaplain, and there would have been visiting masters for writing and possibly French. Music was important, as was dancing, both probably taught by members of the household, and, of course, needlework, at which every lady was expected to be proficient.

The principal adult pastimes at Bradgate were hunting and hawking, but the Dorsets would certainly not have spent the whole year in Leicestershire. The marquess, a man 'neither misliked nor much regarded' by his fellows, was nevertheless one of the leading peers of the realm with political and social duties that would have brought him to London during the winter season, which lasted roughly from November to the beginning of Lent, and although he held no actual office of state under Henry VIII, there would certainly have been other times when it would have been wise for him to be at court. Frances Dorset, too, who was undoubtedly the dominant member of the partnership, liked to keep on the move, paying regular visits to friends and relations such as her cousin Princess Mary, her father and stepmother, now mostly living on their estates in Lincolnshire, or to Dorset's sister Lady Audley or the dowager marchioness at Croydon. To what extent the children were included in these journeyings we do not know, but it seems pretty certain that their eldest daughter would have been introduced to her royal relations at the earliest possible moment. Frances was an ambitious woman, and although disappointed of sons – another daughter, Mary, was born in 1545 – even daughters could be useful in advancing family wealth and status.

By the early 1540s it was looking increasingly unlikely that the king would survive until his son came of age, and already the factions were beginning to jostle for position in the next reign – manoeuvres which inevitably became inextricably involved in the religious and domestic convolutions of the current regime. The progressive party, led originally by Thomas Cromwell and Archbishop Cranmer, which favoured closer links with Lutheran Germany, had suffered a serious setback with the execution of Cromwell in the summer of 1540 – a misfortune usually attributed to Henry's displeasure at being pushed into marriage with his fourth wife, the dowdy German princess Anne of Cleves. It was, of course, rather more complicated than that, but Cromwell, the hard-working, ruthlessly efficient parvenu, had acquired powerful enemies among the conservatives on the Council, led by the old duke of Norfolk and Stephen Gardiner, the right-wing bishop of Winchester, who were only waiting for an opportunity to pounce. The conservatives, too, received an additional stroke of luck just then in the shape of the king's infatuation with Norfolk's teenage niece Katherine Howard, and while her brief ascendancy lasted the Howards and their friends were riding high.

Unhappily for Katherine tales were soon being told, not only of her various premarital sexual flings, but of her very probable adultery with one of the gentlemen of the bedchamber, and after little more than eighteen months as queen she had shared the fate of her cousin Anne Boleyn. The Howards retreated in temporary disarray and the progressives, who now included such up-and-coming men as Prince Edward's uncle Edward Seymour, earl of Hertford, and John Dudley, Viscount Lisle, seemed once more to be enjoying royal confidence – especially since the king's sixth and last wife, the widowed Lady Latymer of Snape Hall, better known by her maiden name Katherine Parr, was also known to favour the friends of the Gospel. But it was never wise to take the king's favour for granted. As long as it seemed politically expedient he had encouraged (or, at any rate, had not seriously discouraged) a certain amount of progressive thinking and had given his blessing to a moderate programme of liturgical reform. He remained, nevertheless, a true conservative at heart and insisted on retaining all the basic elements of Catholicism in his new national Church. These had been set out in the Act of Six Articles, the so-called Whip with Six Strings, which went through parliament in 1539 and made it a capital offence to deny transubstantiation, or the Real Presence in the Eucharist. At the same time communion in one kind for the laity, the celibacy of the clergy, the permanence of vows of chastity, the continuance of private masses and auricular confession were all made mandatory.[17] Henry had also begun to have doubts as to the wisdom of making the English Bible so generally available and another act, for the Advancement of True Religion, was passed in 1543, restricting its use to noblemen and gentlemen, substantial merchants and gentlewomen. This does not seem to have had very much effect for, two years later, in a speech to parliament, the king was 'very sorry to know and hear, how unreverently that most precious jewel the word of God is disputed, rhymed, sung and jangled in every alehouse and tavern, contrary to the true meaning and doctrine of the same'.[18] Generally speaking, though, his policy was to hold a balance between the rival factions and he would, with splendid impartiality, hang Catholics for treason and burn Protestants for heresy. All the same, during the mid-1540s the progressive party looked to be having things pretty much their own way. Very few prosecutions for heresy were brought in 1544 and 1545 and in London especially, the law was being openly flouted.

The climate began to show signs of change in the autumn of 1545. The duke of Suffolk had died in August and his death was held to have been a grievous loss to the reformers. While it is true that the duke had become closely associated with them in recent years, it is not easy to visualise Charles Brandon, that hardbitten old courtier-soldier, in the role of born-again Christian. More plausibly, the impetus behind his patronage of the New Religion can be seen as coming from the duchess. Although still only in her mid-twenties, Catherine Suffolk had developed into a personality to be reckoned with: 'a lady of a sharp wit and sure hand to thrust it home and make it pierce where she pleased'.[19] As well as her sarcastic tongue and a tendency to 'frowardness', much deplored by her masculine acquaintance, my lady of Suffolk possessed a good brain and a lively enquiring intellect, eagerly receptive of new ideas. Together with Margaret Radcliffe, countess of Sussex, Joan Denny, Anne Herbert, Lady Lane, Jane Dudley, Lady Hertford and other like-minded ladies, the duchess of Suffolk had joined an influential group at court which studied and discussed the Gospels and listened to discourses by avant-garde preachers such as Nicholas Ridley, Nicholas Shaxton and Hugh Latimer – a group which met under the sponsorship of the new queen, Katherine Parr.

In spite of their privileged position, the queen and her friends were treading on dangerous ground. Stephen Gardiner and other hard-line bishops, such as Bonner of London, were by no means a spent force and they had an ally in the Lord Chancellor, Thomas Wriothesley. By the end of 1545 they were becoming increasingly disturbed by the spread of religious dissidence, especially in London and the south-east, and had no doubt who to blame for the growing strength of radical views in high places. A vigorous anti-heresy drive was under way by the spring, but Gardiner and Wriothesley remained convinced that the key to the situation lay with the queen, and that the way to bring down the progressives was to attack them through their wives. In the summer of 1546 a promising opportunity presented itself in the person of Anne Kyme, better known by her maiden name of Anne Askew, a notorious heretic already convicted and condemned, who was known to have close connections with the court. Two of her brothers were in the royal service and it seemed highly probable that she had attended some of the queen's bible study sessions – she was certainly acquainted with some of the queen's ladies. If it could be shown that any of these ladies – perhaps even Katherine herself – had been in touch with her since her arrest; if it could be proved that they had been supporting her, then the Lord Chancellor would have ample excuse for an attack on the queen.

Anne was therefore transferred to the Tower and examined by Wriothesley and his henchman the Solicitor General, Richard Rich, about the identity of the other members of her 'sect' but, apart from admitting that she had received small gifts of money from servants wearing the liveries of Lady Denny and Lady Hertford, she told them nothing useful. Exasperated, Wriothesley ordered her to be 'pinched' on the rack. This was not only illegal without a warrant from the Privy Council, it was also counter-productive. Anne either would not or could not (probably could not) provide her tormentors with any further information and, as soon as the story of her ordeal got about, she became a popular heroine.

Having failed with Anne Askew, the queen's enemies were

obliged to fall back on charges of a more general nature, such as the possession of banned books which they felt pretty certain would be found in her apartments, or which could always be planted there. A list of charges had, in fact, been drawn up by early July and the stage set for the queen's arrest. But Henry, who had become sufficiently irritated lately by some of his wife's freely expressed progressive views – she had on one recent occasion been unwise enough to forget that in any debate, especially theological debate, the king must always win hands down – that he had been willing to listen to hints being dropped about her dangerous opinions so 'stiffly maintained'. Now, though, he evidently decided matters had gone far enough and he allowed Katherine to be warned of what was being prepared for her. She quickly seized her chance to explain that she had only been bold enough to seem to engage in argument with her lord and master in order to distract him from the pain of his ulcerated leg and also that she herself might profit from hearing his learned discourse. An affecting reconciliation followed and when Wriothesley arrived with forty yeomen of the guard at his back and a warrant for the queen's arrest in his pocket, he was greeted with a tirade of royal abuse and sent packing with his tail between his legs. This at any rate is the traditional story, as related with much glee and a wealth of circumstantial detail by John Foxe in his best-selling *Book of Martyrs* (reference: John Foxe, Acts and Monuments, ed. S.R. Cattley and G. Townsend, Vol. V, 553–6).

Although Anne Askew went to the stake for her beliefs, her martyrdom and the collapse of the plot against the queen marked the end of the brief conservative resurgence. By the autumn the reactionary Catholic party had suffered a virtual death blow with the disgrace of the duke of Norfolk, followed by the sudden removal of Bishop Gardiner from the list of executors of the king's will. The ruin of the Howards seemed complete. Norfolk's arrogant soldier-poet son, the earl of Surrey, was executed for the technical treason of quartering his arms with those of Edward the Confessor, and the old duke himself only escaped a similar fate by the skin of his teeth. As for Stephen Gardiner, Henry would give no reason for excluding him from the projected Council of Regency, except to say that 'he was a wilful man and not meet to be about his son'.

The motives behind this sudden, savage assault on the conservatives remain somewhat obscure, but one thing is certain – that the driving force came directly from the king. Henry may well have doubted whether either Norfolk or Gardiner, both old-fashioned Catholics at heart, could be trusted to be entirely sound on Royal Supremacy. This was a point on which the king was always ultra-sensitive and may account for the fact that in the closing months of his life he personally ensured that in his son's reign the balance of power would be tilted in favour of those who advocated a more far-reaching programme of church reform than anything he had previously been prepared to countenance; but with men like the earl of Hertford and John Dudley in the driving seat there would at least be no danger of England returning to papal domination.

Edward Tudor and Jane Grey both celebrated their ninth birthdays that autumn: the fair, pretty, clever little boy who would soon have to step into his father's enormous shoes, and the freckle-faced, clever, solemn little girl who was about to become a pawn in the deadly game of power politics played in the grown-up world. For both children childhood was coming to an end and both, in their different ways, were to find the grown-up world a hard and bitter place.

# Two

# As Handsome a Lady
## as Any in England

If I may once get the king at liberty, I dare warrant that
his majesty shall marry no other than Jane.
                                        Thomas Seymour to Lord Dorset

Henry VIII died at Whitehall at about two o'clock in the
morning of Friday 28 January 1547 and at once a curtain
of secrecy descended over the palace as a plan of action,
privately agreed between Edward Seymour, earl of Hertford,
and Secretary of State William Paget, was put into operation.
In his will, a controversial and much-discussed document,
the old king had provided for a council of sixteen executors,
each 'with like and equal charge' to rule the country during
his son's minority – an arrangement so patently impractical
that it had been set aside within a week of his death and at
a meeting of the executors held on 31 January it was agreed
that 'some special man' of their number would have to be
preferred above the rest. The choice was an obvious one and
the council proceeded to confer on Edward Seymour, earl of
Hertford, 'the name and title of Protector of all the realms
and dominions of the King's majesty that now is, and of
Governor of his most royal person'.[1]

There were, of course, plenty of precedents, albeit not
all of them happy ones, for appointing the uncle of a child
king as regent and guardian, and Edward Seymour had

other qualifications. He was a man of proven ability, an experienced and successful soldier and diplomat, generally respected by his peers and trusted by the late king. But he was not of the blood royal, nor even of noble blood. The son of a Wiltshire landowning family, he owed his earldom in part to his own ability but rather more to the fact that his sister had had the good fortune to become queen and give birth to the longed-for male heir. His elevation now to vice-regal status would inevitably give rise to jealousy and faction, and it remained to be seen whether he possessed the qualities necessary to fight off competition and stay at the top of the heap.

He had begun well. Guided by his friend and ally, that shrewd political operator William Paget, Seymour had left the palace before the old king's body was cold. His destination was Hertford Castle, the current residence of the new king; his purpose to get possession of his nephew while Paget handled his interests in London. Largely thanks to Paget, the coup was so skilfully managed that by the time the executors met on the 31st they were simply rubber-stamping an already accomplished transference of power. That same day Seymour brought young Edward to the capital, and saw him safely installed in the fortress palace of the Tower, where his apartments had been 'richly hung and garnished with rich cloth of arras and cloths of estate as appertaineth unto such a royal King'. On the following day came his formal introduction to 'the most part of his nobility, as well spiritual as temporal', who had gathered in the presence chamber to kiss his hand and hear the official promulgation of Seymour's appointment.

The assembled lords then declared they would be ready at all times 'with their might and power' to defend the realm and the king and finally 'cried all together with a loud voice, "God save the noble King Edward!"' After which, the noble King Edward took off his cap and recited his piece: 'We heartily thank you, my lords all; and hereafter in all that you shall have to do with us for any suits or causes, you shall be heartily welcome to us.'[2]

Preparations now began for the coronation, which was to take place on 20 February, and on the 18th there was a grand investiture as the new rulers of England made their first experiments in sharing out the sweets of power. The earl of Hertford was created duke of Somerset to emphasise the grandeur of his position; the queen's brother, William Parr, became marquess of Northampton; John Dudley, Viscount Lisle, became earl of Warwick; and the younger Seymour brother, Thomas, became Baron Seymour of Sudeley. On the 19th Edward made the recognition procession from the Tower to Westminster. Dressed in white and silver, with the tall imposing figure of the new duke of Somerset at his side, the third Tudor king rode through gaily decorated, freshly gravelled streets lined with cheering crowds and surrounded by all the pomp and panoply amassed by his ancestors. The city had, as usual, put on a splendid show, with allegorical tableaux, singing boys and Latin orations at every corner; but as far as Edward was concerned, the high spot of the occasion was undoubtedly the Spanish acrobat who performed 'masteries' on a rope stretched above St Paul's churchyard, and who delayed the king's majesty with all his train 'a good space of time'.[3]

The coronation ceremony itself, performed by Edward's godfather, Archbishop Cranmer, went without a hitch, though it was perhaps ironical that the first king of England to be crowned as Supreme Head of the Church, God's vice-regent and Christ's vicar within his own dominions should have been a child of nine. But if anyone in the congregation found anything even faintly ludicrous in the spectacle they were careful not to say so, and in sermon after sermon preached in the weeks following the coronation Edward was compared to such Old Testament heroes as David, Josiah and the young Solomon. The physical age of the spiritual father of the people was immaterial, his extreme youth a mere temporary inconvenience. What mattered was the fact that he was God's anointed, divinely ordained to guide the people into the paths of righteousness. Edward certainly believed this. Whatever inner misgivings he may have felt were connected not with God's purposes but with man's.

The king's stepmother had been left with no say in the government or in Edward's further upbringing, but the queen dowager was generously provided for in her husband's will. Katherine Parr was now an extremely wealthy lady, and until the king married she would remain the first lady in the land, taking precedence even over the two princesses. Once the coronation was over she moved out to the royal manor at Chelsea, one of her dower houses, a comfortable, up-to-date, red-brick building, convenient for London and pleasantly situated overlooking the Thames on the site of the present Cheyne Walk. She was accompanied by the thirteen-year-old Princess Elizabeth, and on an unrecorded date during that spring or early summer the establishment was also joined by young Jane Grey.

The custom of 'placing out' – that is, of sending one's children away to learn virtue and good manners in a family better circumstanced than one's own – was an old one and much deprecated by foreigners who considered it to be yet another instance of English coldness and selfishness. It seems to have had its origins in the feudal practice of sending a boy to serve as a page in his lord's household as the first step in his progression towards knighthood, while for girls, even if in some cases they paid for their keep by performing domestic duties or acting as 'waiting gentlewomen' to their hostesses, it offered a useful opportunity for acquiring extra accomplishments and social polish, as well of course as enhancing their chances of making a good marriage.

For a girl of Jane Grey's social status the only possible 'place' was the royal household and in normal times she would no doubt have joined the ranks of the queen's maids of honour. As things were, the queen dowager's household would have offered the next best thing. Edward was known to be very fond of his stepmother and although she had no share in the regency Katherine continued to command a great deal of influence and respect. For Jane herself the change in her circumstances brought nothing but good. She had not been happy at home and her parents, her mother in particular, never appear to have shown her any affection. Not that this was necessarily unusual, though the Dorsets do seem to have been rather more unfeeling than most – unless it is simply that their harshness has been better publicised. But the sixteenth century practised no sentimental cult of childhood. Even that enlightened scholar Luis Vives disapproved of 'cockering', or indeed of any outward display of maternal love, 'lest the children become emboldened to do whatever they like'. He was of the opinion that daughters especially should be handled without cherishing, for while indulgence was bad for sons 'it utterly destroyeth daughters'.[4] It is unlikely that Frances Dorset, a buxom, hard-riding woman who, as she grew older, began to bear an unnerving resemblance to her late uncle Henry, had ever read Vives's somewhat turgid manual on *The Education of a Christian Woman*, but she would certainly have agreed with this precept, and her daughters, at least, were never in danger of being destroyed by indulgence.

The queen was a very different proposition. Katherine Parr, like Jane Seymour, came from a well-to-do landed gentry family but possessed neither royal nor noble blood. The Parrs were originally from Kendal in the remote and rugged northern border country of Westmorland, but by the time of Katherine's birth in 1512 they had transferred themselves to the more congenial climate of the English midlands. Katherine's parents were both closely connected with the court, her mother having been a lady-in-waiting and close friend of the unfortunate Catherine of Aragon, and it is possible, though by no means certain, that

Katherine spent some part of her childhood at court and may even have been one of the hand-picked young girls who shared lessons with the Princess Mary. More likely she was brought up with her Parr cousins in Northamptonshire while her mother, widowed at twenty-two, was busy scheming to arrange suitable marriages for the three children she had been left to provide for. Most of the money went on securing an aristocratic bride for William, the only son, so that sixteen-year-old Katherine had to be content with Edward Borough of Gainsborough in Lincolnshire. It was a respectable if not very distinguished match and young Edward was said to be delicate. In fact the marriage lasted no more than about three years. Edward Borough died early in 1533 and Katherine found herself alone in the world at the age of barely twenty-one. Her mother was dead by this time, her brother still a minor and her younger sister still unmarried. Her in-laws showed no inclination to go on giving her a home and as a childless widow she had very little claim on them. It was not a comfortable situation to be in, but Katherine, intelligent, energetic and physically attractive, was soon able to move on and within a year had married again, this time to a kinsman of her father, John Neville, Lord Latymer, of Snape Castle in the North Riding of Yorkshire.

Although he was twice her age and himself twice widowed, being left with two children, Katherine's second marriage seems to have been reasonably successful – at any rate for the first few years. Then in 1536 came the so-called Pilgrimage of Grace, in which various social and economic grievances connected with land title were combined with conservative resentment over religious change and the dissolution of the monasteries to produce the most serious challenge to central government yet seen in the Tudor century. Its effect on the family at Snape was calamitous, as the rebels first seized Lord Latymer as their hostage and spokesman and later, while he was in London protesting that he had been acting under duress against his will, they returned to threaten Katherine and the children. Although the authorities remained deeply suspicious of Latymer, who was known to have conservative sympathies, he escaped the fate of the other defeated rebels but he and his marriage never fully recovered from the experience.

Katherine was now spending more and more of her time in London, where she had already begun to make friends among the 'new-religionists' as they were known – the term Protestant did not come into general use in England until the middle of the century – although she also renewed her childhood acquaintance with the unswervingly Catholic Princess Mary. Lord Latymer died in March 1543 and his widow was soon being courted by the king's brother-in-law, the dashingly handsome Thomas Seymour. It was at this point that the king declared an interest and Seymour melted hastily into the background, leaving Katherine reluctantly to accept the fact that it was plainly God's will that she should become queen of England.

Reluctant though she may have been, Katherine Parr was to prove one of the most satisfactory of Henry's wives. Certainly she was the most likeable, and gave the king loyal and sympathetic companionship during the last years of his life. At thirty-one she was still a pretty woman, but more to the point she was also a mature, well-educated and thoughtful woman, anxious to be a good stepmother as well as a good wife, taking a constructive and affectionate interest in the welfare of her husband's oddly assorted brood. She and Mary were already friends – there was only four years' difference in their ages – and the two younger children responded eagerly to her warmth and kindness. Little Prince Edward was soon writing to her as 'dearest mother' and no one was surprised when Elizabeth was entrusted to the queen's care after her father's death.

Widowed for the third time, Katherine was at long last free to please herself, making no secret of her delight when, very soon after Henry's death, Thomas Seymour renewed his attentions. 'I would not have you to think that this mine honest good will toward you to proceed from any sudden motion of passion,' she wrote to him from Chelsea, 'for truly as God is God, my mind was fully bent, the other time I was at liberty, to marry you before any man I know.'[5] Although she spoke rather half-heartedly about observing a decent period of mourning, Seymour, who had his own reasons for wanting to avoid delay, experienced very little difficulty in cajoling her out of her scruples, and they were married very privately probably no later than May 1547.

Katherine certainly deserved a chance of happiness. The pity was that she had not made a better choice. Thomas Seymour was a fine figure of a man with a commanding presence and plenty of surface charm: 'fierce in courage, courtly in fashion; in personage stately, in voice magnificent, but somewhat empty of matter'.[6] He was also, unfortunately, a vain, greedy, selfish man, consumed with ambition but lacking any political judgement, obsessively jealous of his elder brother and currently labouring under an acute sense of grievance. As well as his peerage and a seat on the Council, he had been given the office of Lord Admiral, passed on to him by John Dudley, but he was very far from being satisfied. An arrangement which allowed one of the king's uncles to enjoy all the fruits of their valuable relationship while leaving the other to be fobbed off with mere consolation prizes seemed to him highly unjust and he had every intention of redressing the balance as soon as he was in a position to do so. His marriage to Katherine had been a first step in this direction – although a rumour was already going round that if my lord 'might have had his own will' he would have married the Lady Elizabeth before he married the queen.

His lordship also had his eye on Lady Jane Grey who, thanks to her great-uncle Henry's will, had now become quite an important little girl. A third Act of Succession, passed in 1544, had confirmed the king's right to dispose of the crown by will, but at the same time made it clear that should Edward die without heirs, and failing any children of the Katherine Parr marriage, the throne was to pass first to Mary and her children and then to Elizabeth, subject to certain conditions to be laid down by their father in his will. The will itself, which was to be a contributory cause of much grief, bitterness and confusion in time to come, recapitulated the provisions of the 1544 Act and went on to stipulate that if either Mary or Elizabeth (neither of whom, incidentally, had been re-legitimated) were to marry without the consent of their brother or his Council, they would forfeit their restored places in the succession. Should the direct line fail altogether, the crown was to come not to the descendants of Henry's elder sister Margaret, who had married the king of Scotland, but instead 'to the heirs of the body of the Lady Frances our niece, eldest daughter to our late sister the French Queen lawfully begotten; and for default of such issue of the body of the said Lady Frances, we will that the said imperial crown . . . shall wholly remain and come to the heirs of the body of the Lady Eleanor, our niece, second daughter to our said late sister the French Queen'.[7]

Only if both Frances and Eleanor failed to leave surviving issue would the imperial crown 'wholly remain and come to the next rightful heirs', unspecified but presumably the royal Stewarts, currently represented by Margaret Tudor's granddaughter Mary Queen of Scots, born in 1542. The motive for this deliberate and apparently perverse act of discrimination against the Scottish line has been attributed to Henry's determination to prevent his realm from falling into the hands of the kings of Scotland. There was also, of course, the common law decree that no foreigner could wear the English crown, but there is not much doubt that the king had been heavily influenced by personal prejudice when drawing up his will. He had been on bad terms with his sister Margaret for several years before her death and in

1544 was still seething over the malice, perfidy and wicked ingratitude of the Scots in refusing to deliver their little queen into his hands as a bride-to-be for Prince Edward.

In 1547, though, the various eventualities provided for in the old king's will still looked reasonably remote. Everyone naturally hoped that Edward would grow rapidly to manhood and prove more fortunate than his father when it came to getting male heirs. Equally naturally any reference to the poor survival record of Tudor boys was taboo in polite society, where the new king was being hailed as a miracle of precocity, learning, gravity and wit, and the most immediate consequence of Henry VIII's eccentric testamentary arrangements was the enhanced social and dynastic status conferred on the children of Frances and Eleanor Brandon. Neither sister had succeeded in raising a son. Like Frances, Eleanor had lost her boy babies and did not herself long survive her uncle, dying in November 1547 at the age of twenty-eight, leaving a seven-year-old daughter, Margaret Clifford, as her only posterity, so that Jane Grey now stood presumptively third in line for the throne. Although very small for her age, and no great beauty with her red hair and freckles, she was apparently quite healthy – a bright, promising child who had become an object of sudden interest to a predator such as Thomas Seymour.

According to the testimony of John Harington, a trusted friend and confidential servant of the new Lord Admiral, he was sent to open negotiations with the marquess of Dorset and use 'all the persuasions he could' to get Dorset to agree to put Jane's future in his master's hands, promising that the Admiral would see her placed in marriage much to her father's comfort. When his lordship seemed 'somewhat cold' and asked for more details, Harington, at least according to his later recollection, replied discreetly that Jane was 'as handsome a lady as any in England, and that she might be wife to any prince in Christendom', and that, if the king's majesty, when he came of age, should decide to marry within the realm, he was as likely to choose his cousin as anyone else. In any case, living in the Lord Admiral's house, who was the king's uncle, must surely increase her chances.[8]

Lord Dorset was to remember the conversation rather differently, declaring that Harington had given him a firm guarantee that the Admiral would arrange to marry his daughter to the king – 'fear you not but he will bring it to pass' – and there seems no reason to doubt that it was on this understanding that a bargain was presently struck and 'certain covenants' entered into. Put crudely, the marquess agreed to sell his daughter's wardship and marriage to Thomas Seymour for the sum of £2,000; the Admiral handed over a few hundred on account and Jane passed into his custody.

It is not entirely clear when this transaction was concluded. According to Dorset, he was first approached 'immediately after the King our late master's death',[9] so it is possible that Jane was already the Admiral's ward living in his town house, Seymour Place, at the time of his marriage to Katherine. Whatever the actual sequence of events, Jane's own preferences were not likely to have been consulted, nor would she have expected them to be. Certainly she was not complaining, for under her new guardians' roof she was enjoying the novel experience of being treated like a favoured guest, petted by the ladies, her 'towardness' openly discussed and admired, her brilliant prospects whispered over. In this congenial atmosphere she naturally began to blossom and to absorb the queen's brand of evangelical Lutheranism with all the eager response to be expected from an intelligent, sensitive child previously starved of affection, encouragement and mental stimulus.

Under the new regime Katherine was no longer obliged to conceal the distinctly left-of-centre religious convictions set out in her own words in her book *Lamentation of a Sinner*, published in the autumn of 1547, in which she confesses how once she had called superstition, godly meaning, and true holiness, error. But now she felt herself to have come, as it were, 'in a new garment before God', who had opened her eyes and made her see and behold Christ, the wisdom of God, the light of the world, 'with a supernatural sight of faith'. All the pleasures, vanities, honours and riches of the world had begun to seem worthless as she came to perceive that Christ was her only saviour and redeemer, 'and the same doctrine to be all divine, holy and heavenly, infused by grace into the hearts of the faithful, which can never be attained by human doctrine, wit, nor reason'.[10]

While Jane was undoubtedly greatly influenced by the queen's piety, she was also now being launched on a programme of studies which included Greek and modern languages as well as Latin. Dr Harding had been superseded by John Aylmer, a protégé of her father, who had paid for the young man's university education and employed him at Bradgate as chaplain and tutor to the children. Aylmer had joined the household in about 1543, though it is not clear if he accompanied Jane when she first went to London. Very probably he did, but in any case Katherine would certainly have taken a close interest in her progress.

The notion that girls as well as boys should be given the chance to benefit from a classical academic education was of comparatively recent origin, being a by-product of that great rebirth – or renaissance – of intellectual curiosity which had first sprung to life in fourteenth- and fifteenth-century Italy and spread slowly northward. Paradoxically the New Learning, as it became known in England, had its roots in a nostalgia for the past. Like most reformers the renaissance scholars wanted to go back to the beginning; to revive the classical culture of the ancient world and, as the movement gained strength in northern Europe, to return to the purity of the Apostolic Church. They turned to the study of Greek partly to rediscover the pre-Christian philosophers but also to be able to read the Gospels in their original form, so that the New Learning had helped to open the door to the New Religion. In England, too, the new wave of scholars had always shown a particular interest in education. Men like William Lily of *Lily's Latin Grammar*, John Colet, founder of St Paul's school, Thomas Linacre the physician, William Grocyn the Greek scholar and Thomas More the lawyer, who congregated in London and Cambridge in the early 1500s, were all eager to disseminate their ideas for the introduction of a wider and more liberal curriculum in the schools and universities, but it was Thomas More, using his own daughters as guinea pigs, who conducted the first serious experiment with the novel idea that girls could be educated too.

By no means everyone was convinced that this was either wise or feasible. Even the great humanist scholar Desiderius Erasmus, More's old friend and admirer, had been sceptical. But the Sage of Rotterdam was so impressed by the mini-Utopia of More's household – 'Plato's Academy on a Christian footing', as he described it, where the great man's daughters studied Latin and Greek, logic, philosophy and theology, mathematics and astronomy – that he was quite won over and predicted that their example would be imitated far and wide. It was not, of course. Highly educated women remained in a small elite minority and even the most advanced educational theorists never dreamt of challenging society's two basic assumptions: that a woman's place was in the home and that a nice girl's only ambition should be to make an honourable marriage and become a good wife and mother. Indeed, the educational theorists from Luis Vives downwards all attached great importance to the housewifely arts. Vives himself was insistent that girls should be taught to handle wool and flax, which were, in his opinion, the two crafts yet left of the old innocent world, and believed 'in no wise that a woman should be ignorant of those feats that must be done by hand, no, not though she be a princess or a queen'.[11]

Katherine Parr may or may not have learnt to spin

wool and flax, but she would certainly have been familiar with the mysteries of household management, and in the *Lamentation of a Sinner* had reminded her own sex to 'learn of St Paul to be obedient to their husbands, to keep silence in the congregation and to learn of their husbands at home'. But this did not mean that she was not strongly in favour of education for her own sex. She had encouraged Princess Mary to exercise her mind and make use of her Latin by embarking on a translation of Erasmus's paraphrase of the Gospel of St John and had taken steps to ensure that Elizabeth was not forgotten in the general reorganisation of the royal schoolrooms which took place in the summer of 1544. Her influence has been detected in the appointment of Richard Cox and John Cheke, both promising young Cambridge humanists, as tutors to the six-year-old Prince Edward, and she would most likely have been responsible for the appointment of William Grindal, also a Cambridge man, as tutor to the Princess Elizabeth.

News of the queen's marriage to Thomas Seymour soon leaked out and by mid-summer he had moved in with his wife, his boisterous loud-voiced personality blowing like a gale through the rather oppressively pious atmosphere of the Chelsea household. The Lord Admiral took no interest in the New Learning and not much in the advancement of the New Religion, his all-consuming interest in the advancement of his own career leaving very little room for anything else. The Admiral wanted to be liked – to be considered a good fellow, generous, open-handed, everybody's friend, was an important part of his image – but his total self-absorption made him a dangerous friend, especially to the weak, the foolish, the young and inexperienced, whom he both fascinated and exploited.

Of the three children in whom he was currently taking an interest, the king was, of course, the most important. Seymour wanted to get the Council to agree to divide the offices of Protector and Governor of the king's person between his brother and himself and, with that end in view, was doing his best to ingratiate himself with his nephew by flattery and surreptitious gifts of pocket money. He had also now begun the questionable practice of bursting in on the Princess Elizabeth in the early morning, still in his nightgown and slippers, to 'bid her good morrow', to tickle her if she was still in bed, or smack her familiarly on the behind and play hide-and-seek around the bed-curtains with her and her maids amid much giggling and squealing. When Elizabeth's governess attempted to remonstrate, he roared that by God's precious soul he meant no evil and would not leave it, adding that the Lady Elizabeth was like a daughter to him. Unable to control either the Admiral or her charge, Mrs Ashley went to the queen for help. Katherine was inclined to 'make a small matter of it', but she promised to accompany her husband in future, and so she did – for a time at least.[12] Just what, if anything, Tom Seymour had hoped to achieve by his teasing pursuit of Elizabeth is difficult to understand. Probably it had begun simply as his idea of a joke; it may well have given him a pleasant sense of power to be on slap-and-tickle terms with Henry VIII's daughter, but he never attempted anything of the sort with Jane Grey who would in any case have been too undeveloped physically for such suggestive romps.

With the approach of autumn relations between the Seymour brothers were showing signs of deterioration. The Lord Protector had not been pleased about Thomas and Katherine's marriage, and now an acrimonious dispute had blown up over some pieces of the queen dowager's jewellery held by the Protector. Katherine claimed these were her personal property, gifts from the late king, but Somerset refused to give them up, insisting they belonged to the Crown. As one of these items was her wedding ring, Katherine's annoyance was understandable. The Protector had also installed a tenant, against her wishes, in one of her dower manors. The normally good-tempered Katherine was furious and threatened to 'utter her choler' to his grace. Nor were family relations improved by the attitude of the Protector's wife. The duchess of Somerset, described as 'a woman for many imperfections intolerable but for pride monstrous',[13] bitterly resented the fact that Katherine as queen dowager was entitled to take precedence over her on state occasions and made no secret of her feelings on the subject. The first parliament of the new reign was due to meet in November and the Admiral, imbued with a fresh sense of his wrongs, stamped about shouting that by God's precious soul he would make this the blackest parliament that ever was in England. When his cronies tried to calm him down, he exclaimed defiantly that he could better live without the Protector than the Protector without him, adding that if anybody went about to speak evil of the queen, he would take his fist to their ears, from the highest to the lowest.[14] Seymour had tried to persuade Edward to write a letter to be presented to the House of Lords requesting them to favour a suit which the Admiral meant to bring before them. This appears to have been connected with his pet scheme to gain custody of the king, but Edward took the advice of his tutor, John Cheke, who said he 'were best not to write', and wisely refused to become involved. Frustrated, the Admiral took to prowling the corridors of St James's Palace, remarking wistfully that he wished the king were at home with him in his house and speculating on how easy it would be to steal the boy away.[15]

In the spring of 1548 scandal threatened to erupt in the family of Katherine and Thomas Seymour. There had been an odd little episode at Hanworth, another of the queen's dower houses a few miles away in Middlesex, when Katherine told Mrs Ashley how the Lord Admiral had looked through the gallery window and seen my Lady Elizabeth cast her arms about a man's neck. The princess denied this accusation tearfully, but Mrs Ashley knew there could be no truth in it, 'for there came no man but Grindal, the

Lady Elizabeth's schoolmaster', who was evidently quite unembraceable. All the same the governess was worried and began to wonder if the queen had invented the story as a hint that she should take better care of the princess 'and be, as it were, in watch betwixt her and my Lord Admiral'.[16] Then, according to a hearsay account given nearly a year after the event, it seems that 'the queen, suspecting the often access of the Admiral to the Lady Elizabeth's grace, came suddenly upon them, when they were alone (he having her in his arms). Wherefore the queen fell out, both with the Lord Admiral and with Her grace also . . . and of this was much displeasure.'[17]

Katherine's initial reaction to this apparent betrayal of her trust by the husband she loved and the girl she had tried to befriend is entirely understandable, especially as she was now five months into a difficult first pregnancy. But although she found some relief in sending for Mrs Ashley and giving that lady a piece of her mind, she could not afford the luxury of giving way to her feelings for long. Gossip, once started, would be unstoppable and a public scandal would be appallingly damaging for everyone concerned. Clearly, though, Elizabeth must be put out of the Admiral's reach as quickly as possible and in the week after Whitsun the princess and her entourage were sent off to pay an extended visit to Sir Anthony Denny and his wife, both old and trusted friends of the royal family, at their house at Cheshunt. The queen and her stepdaughter parted on affectionate terms and thanks to Katherine's generosity and good sense no one, apart from those immediately concerned, was aware of the real reason for the move.

Jane Grey stayed with Katherine and there is nothing to indicate that she was affected in any way by the tensions in her guardians' marriage, or that she missed Elizabeth's companionship. Although the two girls had spent the best part of a year together under the same roof, very likely sharing some of the same lessons and certainly seeing a good deal of one another at meals, at prayers and in general daily intercourse, there is no evidence of any particular friendship having developed between them; nor does there ever appear to have been any correspondence, any exchange of gifts, the loan of a servant with some special skill or indeed any of the small mutual courtesies usual between two young women so closely related. The four-year difference in their ages would, of course, have meant most at the time when they were most in each other's company – the gulf between nine and thirteen can be a wide one – and many years later Henry Clifford, writing the biography of his mistress Jane Dormer, once a maid of honour to Queen Mary Tudor, remarked of Elizabeth that 'a great lady who knew her well, being a girl of twelve or thirteen, told me that she was proud and disdainful, and related to me some particulars of her scornful behaviour, which much blemished the handsomeness and beauty of her person'.[18] There may also have been some jealousy.

Jane Grey might have been only King Henry's great-niece, but no one could cast doubt on her legitimacy or on her mother's virtue, while Elizabeth was still legally the bastard of a notorious adulteress and this fact may well have been mentioned from time to time in the privacy of the household.

On 13 June the queen and the Admiral set out for Sudeley, their Gloucestershire estate, accompanied by a princely retinue and taking Lady Jane with them. Katherine was now more than six months pregnant and a sumptuous nursery had been prepared for the hoped-for son and heir, with enough crimson velvet and taffeta and plate to equip a royal birth. Katherine herself, though obviously aware of the dangers of her approaching childbed – all the more daunting for it being her first at the advanced age of thirty-six – seems to have been happily expectant. Her husband was with her, being unusually attentive, and she had received good wishes from both her royal stepdaughters.

'I trust to hear good success of your grace's great belly,' wrote Princess Mary, 'and in the meantime shall desire much to hear of your health, which I pray almighty God to continue.' Elizabeth had written too, with humble thanks 'that your Grace wished me with you, till I were weary of that country. Your Highness were like to be cumbered, if I should not depart till I were weary of being with you; although it were the worst soil in the world, your presence would make it pleasant.'[19] Katherine also had the pleasure of little Jane Grey's company, and during those quiet summer months in the idyllic surroundings of Sudeley Castle there seems every likelihood that they grew very close to one another.

Katherine's baby arrived on 30 August. It was a girl, christened Mary. The Admiral, who apparently felt no disappointment over the child's sex, at once wrote enthusiastically to his brother with the good news and the Protector responded with a congratulatory note. 'We are right glad to understand that the Queen, your bedfellow, hath had a happy hour; and, escaping all danger, hath made you the father of so pretty a daughter.'[20] Sadly, though, the congratulations were premature, for Katherine developed the dreaded symptoms of puerperal sepsis and within a week she was dead. She was buried in the chapel at Sudeley, the first royal funeral conducted according to the rites of the new religion. Miles Coverdale, the biblical translator, preached the sermon and ten-year-old Jane Grey, a diminutive figure in deepest black, acted as chief mourner for the only person ever to show her disinterested kindness.

As the fever mounted in the last hours of her life, the memory of past hurts came back to torment Katherine and in her delirium she cried out that those about her did not care for her but stood laughing at her grief. Her husband, distressed and embarrassed, tried unsuccessfully to soothe her, but Katherine would only answer 'very roundly and shortly', accusing him of having given her 'many shrewd taunts'.[21] For all his faults Thomas Seymour was not a bad-hearted man and for a while at least seems to have been genuinely stricken by his wife's death. In fact he was 'so amazed' that he almost ceased to care about himself or his doings. He even contemplated breaking up his household and sending Jane Grey back to her parents, but this uncharacteristic loss of confidence soon passed and within a fortnight he was writing to Lord Dorset that, being better advised of himself, he felt that he would after all be able to continue his house together. He continued:

And therefore, putting my whole affiance and trust in God, have begun of new to establish my household, where shall remain not only the gentlewomen of the queen's highness privy chamber, but also the maids which waited at large, and other women being about her grace in her lifetime, with a hundred and twenty gentlemen and yeomen, continually abiding in the house together. . . . And, therefore, doubting lest your lordship might think any unkindness that I should take occasion to rid me of your daughter, the Lady Jane, so soon after the queen's death, for the proof both of my hearty affection towards you, and my goodwill to her, I am minded to keep her until I next speak with your lordship.

His own mother was coming to take charge of the household and would be 'as dear unto her [Lady Jane] as though she were her own daughter', while for his part the Admiral would 'continue her half-father and more, and all that are in my house shall be as diligent about her as yourself would wish'.[22]

This was all very well, but the Dorsets were growing restive. More than a year had gone by with no sign of any of Seymour's 'fair promises' being fulfilled and, although Lord Dorset hastened to thank Lord Seymour for his 'friendly affection' and to assure him that he was still ready to be guided by him in the matter of his daughter's 'bestowing', the marquess was plainly looking for an excuse to wriggle out of his previous undertakings. Jane, he wrote, was too young to be left to rule herself without a guide, and he feared 'lest she should, for lack of a bridle, take too much head' and forget all the good behaviour she had learned from Queen Katherine. His lordship therefore felt strongly that she should be returned to the governance of her mother, by whom she could most easily be 'framed and ruled towards virtue' and her mind, in these so important formative years, addressed to humility, soberness and obedience.[23] Frances Dorset added her voice in a letter enclosed with her lord's in which she, too, thanked her 'good brother' the Admiral for his gentleness but begged him to trust her and to believe that a mother must know what was best for her own child.

This sudden display of concern for their daughter's welfare imperfectly concealed the Dorsets' determination to sell her to the highest bidder and they were, in fact, beginning to wonder whether it might not be wiser to settle for a match with the Protector's son, which had already been tentatively discussed between the families. Jane did go home for a while some time towards the end of September, but John Harington, who was sent to escort her, was of the opinion that she would soon be back and told a colleague that all the maids in the house were hoping for her return.[24]

Harington was quite right in his belief that Jane would be back. She was too valuable a property to be relinquished without a struggle and the Admiral sent another of his henchmen, William Sherington of Lacock Abbey, to work on Frances and himself paid a visit to the Dorsets when, according to the marquess, he was 'so earnestly in hand with me and my wife, that in the end, because he would have no nay, we were contented she should again return to his house', though not, it seems, without much 'sticking of our sides'. During these negotiations, conducted by Lord and

Lady Dorset on one side and Sherington and the Admiral on the other, the Admiral renewed his promise that if he might once get the king at liberty, he would make sure his majesty married none but Jane. He also agreed to advance another £500 of the 2,000 he was 'lending' Jane's parents. There was no need for a bond, declared Thomas Seymour, as the Lady Jane's presence in his house was more than adequate security.[25] The Dorsets, greedy, foolish and chronically hard up, rose to the bait and in October 1548, round about the date of her eleventh birthday, Jane returned to live at Hanworth or Seymour Place in the Strand, under the indulgent chaperonage of old Lady Seymour.

For Jane this was a reprieve. She had written to the Admiral from Bradgate promising that 'like as you have become towards me a loving and kind father, so I shall be always most ready to obey your godly monitions and good instructions, as becometh one upon whom you have heaped so many benefits',[26] but the reprieve was destined to be short. Bereft of Queen Katherine's steadying influence, Thomas Seymour was now openly canvassing support for his schemes to put an end to the Protectorate. He asked Lord Dorset what friends he could count on in his part of the world and advised him to make much of the leading yeomen and freeholders, 'for they be men that be best able to persuade the multitude'. 'Go to their houses', urged the Admiral, 'carrying with you a flagon or two of wine and a pasty of venison, and use a familiarity with them, for so shall you cause them to love you and be assured to have them at your commandment.'[27] He repeated this ingenuous advice to his brother-in-law William Parr, marquess of Northampton, and the young earl of Rutland, telling the latter that he would like to see the king 'have the honour and rule of his own doings'. His lordship did not appear to notice how lukewarm was the response, and when Rutland ventured to remark that he thought the Admiral's power would be much diminished by the queen's death, he brushed this aside impatiently, saying the Council never feared him so much as they did now.[28]

Rutland was not the only one to express doubts about the real strength of the Admiral's powerbase. William Parr was to remember a conversation they had had in the gallery at Seymour Place, when the subject of Jane Grey came up and the Admiral had said that there would be 'much ado' for her, and that the Protector and his wife were trying to get her for their son. But, he went on, 'they should not prevail therein' for her father had given her wholly over to him 'upon certain Covenants that were between them two'. What would he do, asked Northampton, remembering Dorset's reputation for shiftiness, 'if my Lord Protector, handling my lord marquess Dorset gently, should obtain his good will?' 'I will never consent thereunto' was the defiant reply.[29]

The Admiral might have had the law on his side, at least until Jane reached the age of twenty-one, but as far as her marriage was concerned he was no nearer to getting his hands on Edward than he had ever been. Elizabeth, too, remained out of his reach. But in the princess's household, now established at the old bishop's palace at Hatfield, there was excited speculation about his intentions and a rumour had begun to circulate that the real reason why the Lord Admiral had kept Queen Katherine's ladies together was to wait on the Lady Elizabeth after they were married. Rather less credibly, gossip was also linking his name with Lady Jane – a titbit which his lordship passed on to one of his cronies as a joke: 'I tell you this merrily.'

Other people, including the venerable and much-respected Lord Privy Seal, John Russell, tried to warn Seymour of the risks he was running – especially over his increasingly obvious interest in Elizabeth. Any man who sought to marry either of the princesses would undoubtedly 'procure unto himself the occasion of his utter undoing' declared Lord Russell, but Thomas Seymour, who was so closely related to the king, would be particularly vulnerable, for if one of his uncles married one of the heirs to his throne, Edward would be bound to think the worst, and 'as often as he shall see you, to think that you gape and wish for his death'.[30]

But Thomas Seymour, who, for whatever reason, apparently believed himself to be fireproof, persisted on his unwise chosen course. He was now making detailed enquiries into the state of Elizabeth's finances. Thomas Parry, her steward or 'cofferer', came up to London shortly before Christmas and the Admiral took the opportunity to have several conversations with him. He wanted to know all about the size of the princess's household staff; the whereabouts and value of her landed property; what terms she held them on; and, especially, whether or not her title to them had yet been confirmed by letters patent. She could get her lands exchanged for better ones, he told Parry, and wished they were situated in Wales or the West Country – significantly where most of his own strength lay. He went on to ask about her housekeeping expenses and to compare them with 'what was spent in his own house'.[31] He was also sending her friendly messages and even suggesting that he might come and visit her in the country, although when the Protector heard of this he threatened to clap his brother in the Tower if he went anywhere near the princess.

The end of the year approached and with it came the end of the Lord Admiral's enterprising career. The government had put up with a good deal from Thomas Seymour but by early 1549 the evidence of his various 'disloyal practices' had become too circumstantial to be disregarded any longer, and late in the evening of 17 January he was arrested at Seymour Place. Next day the Council's agents began the business of rounding up his associates. The Lady Elizabeth's governess and steward were taken away for questioning and Sir Robert Tyrwhit arrived at Hatfield with instructions to extract a 'confession' from the princess. This proved to be a thankless task. Elizabeth denied and went on denying that either she or her servants had ever at any time contemplated her marriage to the Admiral, or anyone else for that matter, without the consent of the king, the Council and the Lord Protector. Details of those early morning romps at Chelsea and Hanworth, even the shameful reason why Queen Katherine had had to send her away the previous year, were dragged out of Parry and Mrs Ashley but, although embarrassing, these were not evidence of conspiracy and no trick of the interrogator's trade could trap the princess into making any damaging admissions. Even at fifteen Elizabeth Tudor knew how to look after herself.

Gathering evidence of the Admiral's other subversive activities presented fewer problems. William Sherington, who, in his capacity of vice-treasurer of the Bristol mint, had been supplying his lordship with cash derived from clipping the coinage and illicitly buying up and minting church plate, made a full confession, as did John Fowler of the Privy Chamber, who had been acting as Seymour's private intermediary with the king. Even the king himself obligingly remembered certain conversations he had had with his uncle over the past two years, while the marquess of Dorset, in a series of self-exculpatory statements, was busy helping the government with its enquiries, explaining how he had been 'seduced and aveugled' against his better judgement into cooperating with Seymour's plans for his daughter's future. The only person who attempted to speak up for the Admiral was his friend John Harington, who deposed that he had heard his master say of the Lady Jane 'that she should not be married until such time as she should be able to bear a child, and her husband able to get one'.[32]

The Council met on 22 February to consider the matter and came to the conclusion that 'the Lord Admiral was sore charged of divers and sundry Articles of High Treason . . . against the King's Majesty's person and his Royal Crown'. Thirty-three Articles or charges had been drawn up in the form of an indictment and since parliament was then in session it was agreed that any further proceedings should take the form of a bill of attainder – always a cheap and convenient method of dealing with troublemakers. This passed both Houses early in March and it now lay with the Protector to take the final decision on his brother's fate. There was silence for nearly a week while, presumably, the unfortunate Somerset wrestled with his conscience. Then the earl of Warwick, who had been quietly waiting for the Seymour brothers to destroy each other, applied some discreet pressure on his fellow councillors, who waited on the king with a request that they might 'proceed to justice' without further troubling him or the Lord Protector. Edward, who did not greatly care for either of his uncles, raised no objection and the Admiral went to keep his appointment with the executioner on Tower Hill on 20 March.[33]

There can, of course, be no reasonable doubt that Thomas Seymour had wanted to marry Elizabeth, that he would have liked to overthrow his brother's government and that he had actively plotted to achieve both these objectives but whether the Imperial ambassador was right in assuming that 'following the example of Richard III he wished to make himself king' is another matter altogether. The younger Seymour was an unstable, irresponsible character who had allowed his personal jealousy and ambition to become obsessions, but such an inept conspirator scarcely represented a very serious danger to the state. He did, however, represent a serious nuisance which could no longer be safely tolerated.

Jane Grey had played no part in any of these dramatic events. She had been hastily removed by her parents at the time of the Admiral's arrest and was now back at Bradgate, well out of harm's way. What her feelings were are not recorded, nor how much she knew of the details, but she would undoubtedly have heard all about the last moments of the man who had once been towards her a 'loving and kind father'. It seemed that Thomas Seymour had died badly, refusing, as he stood on the scaffold, to exhibit the Christian contrition and resignation considered proper on such occasions. His execution, too, was badly botched and it took two strokes of the axe to kill him, but, as Hugh Latimer remarked in his funeral sermon, 'when a man hath two strokes with an axe who can tell but that between two strokes he doth repent'. Bishop Latimer refused to speculate further, only saying, in a sermon not noticeably pervaded with the spirit of Christian charity, that he had died very dangerously, irksomely and horribly. It seemed, in fact, as if God had clean forsaken the Lord Admiral and the bishop felt the realm was well rid of him. 'He was, I heard say, a covetous man: I would there were no more in England . . . a seditious man, a contemner of common prayer: I would there were no more in England. Well, he is gone: I would he had left none behind him!'[34] But Tom Seymour had left his infant daughter behind him, an innocent and often forgotten victim of the whole sorry affair. Little Mary Seymour, orphaned at seven months, was, at her father's request, handed over to the reluctant care of the duchess of Suffolk, once her mother's dear friend, and is believed to have died about the time of her second birthday.[35]

Down at Hatfield Elizabeth was already embarking on the campaign to clear her name, addressing one of her carefully crafted letters to the Lord Protector in which she asked that a proclamation declaring that the tales being spread about her 'were but lies' should be issued to silence the gossip-mongers. The Protector was not unsympathetic but he had more serious concerns than the princess's reputation on his mind in the summer of 1549, which was marked by widespread and increasing popular discontent. On Whit Sunday the first English Book of Common Prayer, the fruit of Thomas Cranmer's labours over the past decade, became the only legal form of worship. Based on the traditional Sarum rite, the new liturgy remained something of a compromise between old and new, and was worded loosely enough, it was hoped, to be acceptable to all but the most entrenched conservatives. Nevertheless its launch led to angry rejection by clergy and parishioners in parts of the Home Counties, followed by a quite serious armed rebellion in the West Country, where the prayer book was ungratefully dismissed as no more than a 'Christmas game'. Another, more serious, rising broke out in East Anglia in July. This was due less to religious outrage than to economic grievances connected with the enclosure of common land and aroused correspondingly serious alarm in the minds of the landowning classes.

The Protector's possibly not-altogether-deserved reputation for sympathy with the poor and their troubles might have earned him the title of 'the Good Duke' among some sections of the populace, but it did nothing to endear him to his peers, who turned instead towards the earl of Warwick, a reassuringly tough and capable soldier, untroubled by any dangerous notions about social justice. Meanwhile, Somerset's growing sense of isolation and insecurity was being reflected in a show of arrogance and intolerance of opposition – 'great choleric fashions whensoever you are contraried' – which had the effect of alienating his remaining support on the Council. His public image, too, had been badly damaged by his brother's death, just as Warwick had known it would be. His outwardly unfeeling acceptance of the Admiral's execution had repelled a lot of people who now, unfairly, stigmatised him as a fratricide, 'a bloodsucker and a ravenous wolf'.

In mid-September the earl of Warwick returned to London in triumph after successfully destroying the East Anglian rebels at Dussindale. As well as being the hero of the hour, he had a well-armed, experienced body of troops at his disposal and judged the moment was now ripe for an attempt to dislodge the Protector. Towards the end of the month the citizens were surprised to see the lords of the Council going armed about the streets with their servants 'likewise weaponed, attending upon them in new liveries, to the great wondering of many'. There was much coming and going at Warwick's house in Holborn and rumours that 'the confederates in this matter' were planning to seize the Tower went flying round the town.[36]

Somerset was at Hampton Court with the king, trying ineffectually to raise some support in the neighbourhood, when he heard that the 'London Lords', as the opposition had become known, intended to pay him an unfriendly visit. On Saturday 6 October, between nine and ten in the evening, he got Edward out of bed and bundled him off to seek sanctuary at Windsor – an unnerving experience for which the king never really forgave him. But Warwick and his confederates pursued him there and a few days later the Lord Protector had surrendered and was conveyed under arrest to the Tower. It was not, as might have been expected, the final disaster. The 'Good Duke' still had quite a considerable popular following, both in London and elsewhere, and Warwick was far too astute to risk overreaching himself at this stage. Somerset was presently released, even temporarily regaining a seat on the Council, but his reign was over and his end merely postponed.

The new strong man was in his late forties with a commanding presence and magnetic personality, whose career had followed the perfect pattern for the rise of the Tudor meritocracy. The Dudleys were a respectably old baronial family, deriving their surname from the castle and town in the West Midlands, but John was descended from a junior branch of the tree and his father Edmund, a clever lawyer with a first-class financial brain, had served Henry VII in the capacity of fiscal adviser rather too efficiently for his own good. One of the first acts of the young Henry VIII had been to offer Edmund Dudley, together with his colleague Richard Empson, as sacrifices on the altar of public opinion and both men were executed on charges which the government scarcely bothered to pretend were other than contrived to appease the outraged taxpayers of England. John Dudley, who was nine years old at the time, became the ward of his father's friend Edward Guildford, a prosperous landowner in Kent and Sussex, and he later married his guardian's daughter.

A darkly handsome boy, gifted, forceful and ferociously ambitious, young John was clearly destined to be a high-flyer and by the early 1520s had begun to make a name for himself in military circles. He was knighted by the duke of Suffolk during the brief and not very glorious French expedition of 1523, while his spectacular feats of courage and skill in the tiltyard earned him royal esteem and the sort of glamour normally associated with a sporting superstar. By the next decade he had progressed to more serious things, proving that he could also offer a wide range of political, diplomatic and administrative talents in total commitment to the king's service. In 1542 he was entrusted with the responsible job of Warden of the Scottish Marches and was raised to the peerage as Viscount Lisle – a title devolving from his mother, born Elizabeth Grey, aunt of that other Elizabeth Grey once briefly betrothed to Charles Brandon. (It is always useful to remember that the Tudor ruling class comprised a very small and intricately interrelated society.) During the remainder of the 1540s he continued to enhance his reputation as a first-rank military commander and his name had, of course, figured high on the magic list of executors of King Henry's will.

Throughout his career Warwick had made a careful study of Tudor psychology and he had become a particular favourite with the old king, especially after the death of Charles Brandon. His plan in the winter of 1549/50 seems to have been to use the still malleable Edward as a screen behind which further to consolidate his own position and secure the future of his numerous sons. In private life the earl was an affectionate family man with plenty of experience of bringing up boys, but he never made the mistake of treating Edward like a child. Instead he treated him as a king, who would soon be old enough to start taking an active part in the business of government, and Edward at just twelve years old responded eagerly to this carefully calculated form of flattery.

The success of the second bloodless coup of the reign had been due largely to the Protector's lack of tact and judgement, and his failure to foresee and control the social unrest resulting from religious change, economic hardship and the unpopular policy of enclosure; he also made the serious tactical mistake of giving Warwick the chance to take the credit for suppressing the rebels at Dussindale. In retrospect it all looks so easy, but it could just as easily have gone either way. If John Russell, who had just dealt successfully with the western rising, and the marquess of Northampton had sided with Somerset the outcome could well have been different. One thing though is surely not in question: the Lord Protector's fall had made the tragedy of Jane Grey inevitable.

# THREE

# THIS MOST NOBLE VIRGIN

It is incredible how far she [Jane] has advanced already,
and to what perfection she will advance in a few years
. . . unless perhaps she is diverted from her pursuits by
some calamity of the times.

John Ulmer to Conrad Pellican

In the late summer of 1550 Mr Roger Ascham was
travelling south from his Yorkshire home en route for the
port of Billingsgate, where he was to embark for Germany
on a diplomatic mission to the Emperor Charles V, but
he broke his journey in Leicestershire in order to call at
Bradgate and take his leave of Lady Jane Grey.

Ascham was another Cambridge man, already in his
mid-thirties enjoying a considerable reputation as a scholar
with advanced ideas on the education of the young. He
had been briefly a member of the household at Chelsea,
winning the coveted post of tutor to the Princess Elizabeth
after the death of William Grindal in January 1548, and
had become a great admirer of John Aylmer's star pupil.
He found her that August day 'in her chamber, reading
*Phaedon Phaedonis* in Greek, and that with as much delight
as some gentleman would read a merry tale in Boccaccio'.
When, 'after salutation and duty done', he asked why
she was not with her parents and all the other ladies
and gentlemen who were out hunting in the park, Jane
answered with a smile that she knew all their sport was

but a shadow to the pleasure she found in Plato. 'Alas, good folk, they never felt what true pleasure meant.' 'And how came you, Madame,' enquired Ascham, 'to this deep knowledge of pleasure, and what did chiefly allure you unto it: seeing not many women but very few men have attained thereunto?' Her answer was astonishing:

> I will tell you, and tell you a truth which perchance ye will marvel at. One of the greatest benefits that ever God gave me, is that he sent me so sharp and severe parents and so gentle a schoolmaster. For when I am in presence of either father or mother, whether I speak, keep silence, sit, stand or go, eat, drink, be merry or sad, be sewing, playing, dancing or doing anything else, I must do it, as it were, as perfectly as God made the world, or else I am so sharply taunted, so cruelly threatened, yea presently sometimes with pinches, nips and bobs, and other ways, which I will not name, for the honour I bear them, so without measure misordered, that I think myself in hell, till time come that I must go to Mr Aylmer, who teacheth me so gently, so pleasantly, with such fair allurements to learning, that I think all the time nothing whilst I am with him. And when I am called from him, I fall on weeping, because whatever I do else but learning is full of grief, trouble, fear and whole misliking unto me. And thus my book hath been so much my pleasure and more, that . . . all other pleasures, in very deed, be but trifles and troubles unto me.[1]

Roger Ascham was so deeply impressed by this remarkable outburst, all the more so because it was to be the last conversation they were ever to have, that he remembered and later preserved it for posterity in his famous manual *The Scholemaster*. Ascham used Jane's situation as yet another argument to further his constant plea for the adoption of more humane teaching methods, while generations of Protestant propagandists and hagiographers have used it to illustrate both her praiseworthy addiction to learning and her parents' undeservedly abusive treatment of her. It is only quite recently that biographers have begun to question the received image of gentle Jane, meek and mild – an image largely created for the edification of pupils in Victorian schoolrooms. At thirteen the real Jane Grey was a stubborn, unusually bright, articulate and opinionated adolescent, who apparently did not hesitate to inform sympathetic visitors that she found her parents' company hellish and whose youthful self-righteousness must often have profoundly irritated her father and mother.

Like all their set the Dorsets were compulsive gamblers, playing for high stakes at both cards and dice, a practice much deplored by the godly. James Haddon, the resident chaplain at Bradgate, fought a long losing battle with his employers over this issue, for although quite prepared to forbid their domestics to risk money on amusements of this sort, my lord and his lady with their friends reserved the right not only to play in their private apartments, but to play for money, pointing out, reasonably enough, that the game lost all its interest without a stake, and they turned quite nasty when Haddon reproved them publicly from the pulpit.[2] If, as seems likely, the chaplain was supported by Aylmer and Lady Jane, this would have done nothing to lessen the tensions of family life.

All this time Jane's intellectual and spiritual horizons were continuing to widen and Roger Ascham, with fond recollections of the 'so divine a maid' he had found engrossed in the *Phaedon* of Plato, wrote urging her to: 'Go on thus, O best adorned virgin, to the honour of thy country, the delight of thy parents, the comfort of thy relatives, and the admiration of all.' Ascham was feeling very much out of his element in a quarrelsome Germany, where 'all places and persons are occupied with rumours of wars and commotions', and was frankly envious of Aylmer. 'O happy Aylmer! to have such a scholar and to be her tutor. I congratulate both you who teach and she who learns.'[3]

Ascham himself had taught Elizabeth by his famous method of double translation, presenting her with passages of Demosthenes or Cicero to be turned first into English and then back into their original languages. It seems probable that Aylmer followed a similar plan and Jane would have read all the most approved classical authors plus, of course, the Gospels and the Acts of the Apostles in Greek and the works of the Fathers of the Church such as Cyprian, Jerome and Augustine. Ascham, who had already challenged Jane to write to him in Greek and told his friend John Sturm, the Protestant Rector of Strasburg University that her skill in writing and speaking the language was 'almost past belief', now suggested that if she herself were to take the trouble to write a letter in Greek to Sturm, neither she nor Aylmer would regret it.

Roger Ascham is also sometimes credited with first bringing Jane to the notice of Henry Bullinger, chief pastor of the radical church of Zurich, but her connection with the Continental reformers was actually initiated in the spring of 1550 by John ab Ulmis or Ulmer, an impecunious Swiss student who had come over to England to seek his fortune and contrived to ingratiate himself with the marquess of Dorset, 'the protector of all students and the refuge of foreigners'. This noble personage, Ulmer informed Bullinger, had a daughter, 'pious and accomplished beyond what can be expressed', to whom he intended to present a copy of Bullinger's book on the holy marriage of Christians, and so began a correspondence conducted, naturally, in Latin, which continued sporadically over the next two-and-a-half years.

In July 1551 Jane is thanking Bullinger for sending her father and herself his treatise on Christian Perfection – that little volume of 'pure and unsophisticated religion' from which she is daily gathering the sweetest flowers, as out of a beautiful garden. Her most noble father, she added hastily, would have written himself had he not been so busy with public affairs and will do so as soon as he has leisure from his other weighty engagements. She herself is now beginning to learn Hebrew and would be greatly obliged if Bullinger would point out 'some way and method of pursuing this study to the greatest advantage'.[4]

John Ulmer, who was determined to keep his toehold on the comforts to be enjoyed at Bradgate, had also written to Conrad Pellican, another Swiss reformer, extolling the virtues of his patron's daughter: 'I do not think that among all the English nobility for many ages past there has arisen an individual who to the highest excellence of talent and judgement has united so much diligence and assiduity in the cultivation of every liberal pursuit.' The Lady Jane, it seemed, was not only conversant with the more polite accomplishments and ordinary acquirements, but had also 'so exercised herself in the practice of speaking and arguing with propriety, both in Greek and Latin, that it is incredible how far she has advanced already, and to what perfection she will advance in a few years; for well I know that she will complete what she has begun, unless perhaps she is diverted from her pursuits by some calamity of the times'.[5]

Aylmer and Haddon, meanwhile, had begun writing to Bullinger themselves. In a series of letters, which forms a small part of the vast bulk of his correspondence – the so-called Zurich Letters – they poured out their hopes and fears for their prize pupil and asked for help in the anxious task of guiding her in the paths of learning and piety and away from those temptations of the world, the flesh and the devil, so dangerous for any high-born young girl, but especially one who, for all her rare qualities and virtues, was just a little inclined to be headstrong. 'Although she is so brought up, that there is the greatest hope of her advancement in godliness,' wrote Haddon, Bullinger's exhortations would afford her valuable encouragement, 'and at the same time have their due weight with her, either as proceeding from a stranger, or from so eminent a person as yourself'.[6] At one time Aylmer seems to have been afraid that the teenage Jane was showing signs of taking rather too much interest in her appearance – such unworthy matters as dress, jewels and 'braidings of the hair' – and of spending too much time on her music. 'It now remains for me to request', he wrote solemnly to the middle-aged Swiss pastor, 'that you will instruct my pupil in your next letter as to what embellishment and adornment of the person is becoming in young women professing godliness. . . . Moreover, I wish you would prescribe to her the length of time she may properly devote to the study of music.'[7]

Communication between Leicestershire and Zurich was slow and further impeded by a shortage of reliable messengers, but in another letter from Jane to Bullinger, dated from Bradgate in the summer of 1552, she speaks of the debt of gratitude she owes him. She had read his latest letter twice over and feels she has derived as much benefit from his 'excellent and truly divine precepts' as from her daily study of the best authors. 'You exhort me to embrace a genuine and sincere faith in Christ my Saviour,' she went on, with characteristic cautious honesty. 'I will endeavour to satisfy you in this respect, as far as God shall enable me to do; but as I acknowledge faith to be his gift, I ought therefore only to promise so far as he may see fit to bestow it upon me. I shall not however cease to pray, with the apostles, that he may of his goodness daily increase it in me. . . . Do you meanwhile, with your wonted kindness, make daily mention of me in your prayers. In the study of Hebrew I shall pursue that method which you so clearly point out.'[8]

Despite the gulf of age, background and geographical distance which separated them, this curious penfriendship continued to flourish. 'Were I indeed to extol you as truth requires, I should need either the oratorical powers of Demosthenes, or eloquence of Cicero,' wrote Jane in the third and last of her surviving letters. She herself was painfully conscious of her own inadequacy.

In writing to you in this manner I have exhibited more boldness than prudence: but so great has been your kindness towards me, in condescending to write to me, a stranger, and in supplying the necessary instruction for the adornment of my understanding and the improvement of my mind, that I should justly appear chargeable with neglect and forgetfulness of duty, were I not to show myself mindful of you and of your deservings in every possible way. Besides, I entertain the hope that you will excuse the more than feminine boldness of me, who, girlish and unlearned as I am, presume to write to a man who is the father of learning; and that you will pardon that rudeness which has made me not hesitate to interrupt your more important occupations with my vain trifles. . . . My mind is fluctuating and undecided; for while I consider my age, sex and mediocrity, or rather infancy, in learning, each of these things deters me from writing; but when I call to mind the eminence of your virtues, the celebrity of your character, and the magnitude of your favours towards me, the higher consideration yields to the inferior; a sense of what is becoming me gives way to your worth, and the respect which your merits demand usually prevails over all other considerations. . . . As long as I shall be permitted to live, I shall not cease to offer you my good wishes, to thank you for the kindness you have showed me, and to pray for your welfare. Farewell, learned sir. Your piety's most devoted, Jane Grey.[9]

Much of the flattering interest shown in Jane by the European reformers stemmed from their hopes that she and Edward might yet make a match of it. 'A report has prevailed . . . that this most noble virgin is to be betrothed and given in marriage to the king's majesty,' John Ulmer told Bullinger with more optimism than accuracy in May 1551. 'Oh, if that event should take place, how happy would be the union and how beneficial to the church!'[10] But as the noble virgin approached her fourteenth birthday and with it the end of childhood, she was still unspoken for – since the fall of Protector Somerset nothing more had been heard of a marriage between Jane and his son – and negotiations were currently well advanced for the betrothal of the king of England to the French (and popish) Princess Elisabeth.

In July 1551 tragedy struck the Suffolk Brandons when the two young sons of Charles Brandon by Catherine Willoughby, then undergraduates at Cambridge, died within hours of one another of the sweating sickness. This mysterious disease had first appeared in England in 1485, brought, so it was said, by the French mercenaries who came over with Henry VII, and remained a scourge throughout the first half of the Tudor century, when it suddenly vanished or mutated. The 'sweat', with its symptoms of chills, high fever, severe headache, backache and vomiting, sounds like a virulent form of influenza, but was probably caused by a virus unconnected with any modern strain. It was notorious for the terrifying speed of its onset – a victim could sit down to dinner apparently in the best of health and be dead by suppertime. Nor was it any respecter of persons. On the contrary, the comfortable classes seem to have been most at risk. The deaths of the sixteen-year-old duke of Suffolk and his younger brother, who both appear to have been particularly attractive and promising boys, was a devastating blow to their mother and their loss was widely regarded as a blow to society. As Henry Machyn, the London funeral furnisher, commented in his *Diary*: 'It was great pity of their death, and it had pleased God, of so noble a stock they were, for there is no more left of them.'[11]

Society's loss, however, was to prove the Grey family's gain when, on 4 October 1551, the now-extinct dukedom of Suffolk was recreated as a new peerage and conferred on the marquess of Dorset *jure uxoris*, that is, in right of his wife, the sole surviving heir to the Brandon estates. That October was a crowded month. To no one's great surprise the duke of Somerset was rearrested on the 16th, charged with plotting to overthrow the government of his successor, who now felt sufficiently confident to proceed with Somerset's final disposal. John Dudley had wisely eschewed the title of Protector. England's new strong man was more interested in the realities of power than its trappings but he did now feel the time was ripe to petition the king for a step in rank, and on 11 October he was created duke of Northumberland, making him the first Englishman having no ties either of blood or marriage with the royal family ever to bear a ducal title.

The Greys and the Dudleys had both received their promotion by the time Mary of Guise, the widowed mother of Mary Queen of Scots and Regent of Scotland, on her way home from seeing her young daughter at the French court, became stormbound at Portsmouth and sent word to the king that she would continue her journey overland and wanted to take the opportunity to visit him. The dowager travelled up to Hampton Court, where she was met by an impressive delegation of nobility and gentry, headed by the marquess of Northampton, who escorted her to the palace to be greeted by 'ladies and gentlewomen to the number of threescore, and so she was brought to her lodging on the queen's side, which was all hanged with arras, and so was the hall, and all the other lodgings of mine in the house, very finely dressed'. This was the first state visit which Edward had hosted and he was clearly determined to show that he knew how such things should be done, recording the details minutely in his Journal. That night and the next day, he went on, 'all was spent in dancing and pastime, as though it were a court, and great presence of gentlemen resorted thither'.[12]

After 'perusing' Hampton Court and seeing some deer coursing, Mary continued up to London where she was lodged in the bishop of London's palace. This time the welcoming party was headed by the duke of Suffolk, who brought a message from the king that 'if she lacked anything she should have it, for her better furniture', while the ladies appointed to salute her included the Lady Frances, duchess of Suffolk, 'the Lady Jane daughter to the Duke of Suffolk', and the duchess of Northumberland. On the following day, 4 November, a grand dinner and reception was held in her honour at Westminster. 'In the hall I met her with all the rest of the lords of my council . . . and from the outer gate up to the presence chamber, on both sides, stood the guard,' recorded the fourteen-year-old monarch, a touch complacently. At dinner the Queen Regent sat under the same cloth of estate on the king's left hand, while further down the table were 'my cousin Frances and my cousin Margaret [Douglas]. . . . We were served by two services, two sewers, cupbearers, carvers and gentlemen. Her *maistre d'hotel* came before her service, and mine officers before mine. There were two cupboards [of plate], one of gold four stages [in] height, another of massy silver six stages. . . . After dinner, when she had heard some music, I brought her to the hall, and so she went away.'[13]

The Regent's visit had marked Jane's debut in grown-up society and also seems to have been the only time that Edward mentioned her name in his Journal. For all the optimistic talk of their likely marriage in Protestant circles abroad, there is absolutely no indication that Edward himself, or Jane for that matter, ever considered it even as a remote possibility. Edward, indeed, is said to have declared that his future bride should be a foreign princess 'well stuffed and jewelled'.

Although the Suffolks had been much in evidence at

the Westminster banquet it was noticeable that neither of the Ladies Mary and Elizabeth were among those present and indeed the king's half-sisters played hardly any part in the life of his court. Mary Tudor, now in her mid-thirties, had suffered bitterly as a result of her parents' divorce and still bore the scars of those sufferings. Forcibly separated from her much-loved mother – she had not even been allowed to go to her in her last illness, viciously humiliated by her father's second wife and finally bullied by her father into signing a document repudiating the Bishop of Rome's 'pretended authority' and acknowledging her own illegitimacy, Mary had, not surprisingly, developed into a nervous, unhappy, dyspeptic woman with little taste for socialising. In any case, by the autumn of 1551 the unfortunate princess was once again at loggerheads with the authorities over her religious beliefs.

Trouble had begun in the spring of 1549 with the introduction of Thomas Cranmer's prayer book, replacing the ancient Latin mass with some newfangled communion service. Faced with the threatened proscription of the Catholic faith which had long been her only consolation, Mary had appealed to her powerful kinsman, the Holy Roman Emperor himself, and Charles had responded by demanding a written undertaking from the duke of Somerset that his cousin should be allowed to continue to practise her religion unmolested. This was refused, but Somerset did reluctantly agree that Mary might do as she thought best in the privacy of her own house, at least until such time as the king came of age. But then came the October coup and early in 1550 Mary was warned that her breathing space would soon be over. During that summer a warrant was issued for the arrest of one of her chaplains and by the autumn the battle of the Lady Mary's mass was fairly joined, the government maintaining that any promises made by the former Lord Protector had been strictly temporary and provisional and, in any case, applied only to the princess herself. Certainly the fifty-odd members of her household staff could claim no privileges and must obey the king's law or suffer the consequences. By the following January the king himself had taken a hand in the affair, adding a postscript to one of the Council's hectoring letters: 'Truly, sister,' he wrote, 'I will not say more and worse things, because my duty would compel me to use harsher and angrier words. But this I will say with certain intention, that I will see my laws strictly obeyed, and those who break them shall be watched and denounced.'[14]

This unequivocal statement of Edward's position would have come to Mary as a bitter revelation of the gulf which lay between them. Until now she had been able perhaps to comfort herself with the belief that her little brother was only a helpless tool in the hands of men like John Dudley and his cronies – that it was they, not he, who were her enemies. But in the king's letter the echo of their father's voice was too unmistakable to be denied.

Mary had been avoiding the court deliberately, keeping her occasional visits as brief and as private as possible for fear that she would somehow be tricked or forced into attending one of the new services and so appear to be lending her countenance to the hated New Religion. But in March 1551 she had gone up to town to make a plea for brotherly tolerance and consideration. 'The Lady Mary my sister came to me at Westminster,' recorded Edward with characteristic terseness, '. . . where it was declared how long I had suffered her mass *against my will* [he later crossed these words out] in hope of her reconciliation, and how now . . . except I saw some short amendment, I could not bear it. She answered that her soul was God's and her faith she would not change, nor dissemble her opinion with contrary doings. It was said I constrained not her faith, but willed her not as a king to rule, but as a subject to obey. And that her example might breed too much inconvenience.'[15]

The king took his responsibilities as keeper of his people's conscience with great seriousness, and yet it seems likely that the question of his sister's awkward stance did not at that time worry him too extremely. Mary, by contemporary standards, was already middle-aged. To Edward, at thirteen, she must have seemed already old – she was, after all, more than old enough to be his mother – and her health was known to be poor. Edward, a notably unsentimental child, may well have reflected that the problem would surely soon go away of its own accord and, left to himself, he might well have been prepared, reluctantly, to let the matter rest.

But unhappily for Mary, she was now once again heiress presumptive and her actions and beliefs consequently had political significance. John Dudley had found it expedient, for reasons not unconnected with his regime's increasing financial difficulties, to form an alliance with the radical wing of the Protestant party. At the same time, he was aware that the conservative bulk of the English people disliked the noisy violence of the militant reformers and their spoliation of the parish churches, and that the silent majority agreed in their hearts with the Lady Mary when she wished aloud that everything could have remained as it was at the time of her father's death. Her example and her influence were important and so, as once before, it was necessary to compel her submission and, as once before, Mary surrendered. By the end of the year mass was no longer being celebrated in her chapel where, of course, any of her neighbours who wished to come and worship in the old familiar way had always been welcome. Mary herself continued to seek the consolations of her religion, but in fear and secrecy behind the locked doors of her own apartments.

Edward's relations with his younger sister were uncomplicated by theological divergence, and Elizabeth was always 'most honourably received' when she came to court, in order, reported the Imperial ambassador, 'to show the people how much glory belongs to her who has embraced the new religion and become a very great lady'.[16] All the same, the great lady herself, who had by this time pretty well succeeded in living down the unfortunate effects of the Seymour scandal, was being careful to avoid obvious involvement with any factional interests and keeping her public appearances to a minimum. Her failure to greet Mary of Guise had probably had a good deal to do with the fact that the French were already beginning to insinuate that, as the late king's bastard, she had no right to her place in the succession. Since his domestic policies had brought him into collision with the Emperor, the duke of Northumberland had been forced to cultivate the French and Elizabeth would naturally have been unwilling to run the risk of a snub. She therefore stayed at home, ostentatiously ignoring the interest in French fashions which the Regent's visit had reawakened among her contemporaries. Elizabeth at this time affected a severely plain style of dress which had won her golden opinions among the reforming party. John Aylmer, among others, commented approvingly on her refusal to alter any of her 'maiden shamefastness' or to copy those noblemen's wives and daughters who were going about 'dressed and painted like peacocks'.[17]

Elizabeth was, of course, setting a fashion to be copied by other high-born Protestant maidens. When Jane Grey received a gift from Mary of 'goodly apparel of tinsel cloth of gold and velvet, laid on with parchment lace of gold', she said: 'What shall I do with it?' 'Marry', said a gentlewoman standing by, 'wear it.' 'Nay', answered she, 'that were a shame to follow my Lady Mary against God's word, and leave my Lady Elizabeth, which followeth God's word.'[18] Jane was never exactly noted for her tact.

In spite of the growing religious divide, however, there was far more friendly intercourse between the Suffolk family and the Lady Mary than there was with Elizabeth. Mary Tudor and Frances Suffolk were very much of an age, sharing much the same childhood memories and seeing quite a lot of each other. For instance, it is recorded that in November 1551 Frances and all three of her daughters stayed with Mary for several weeks at the princess's town house, the former Priory of St John of Jerusalem at Clerkenwell, and this may have been the occasion when Mary gave 'my cousin Frances' a pair of beads (that is, a rosary) of crystal trimmed with a tassel of goldsmith's work, and 'to my cousin Jane Gray' a necklace of goldsmith's work and small pearls and another 'lace for the neck' of small pearls and rubies, suitable trinkets for a young girl.[19]

The duke and duchess, their three daughters and the duke's younger brothers, Lord Thomas and Lord John Grey, spent that Christmas at Tylsey, or Tilty, in Essex, home of the Willoughbys of Woollaton. The duke's aunt, Lady Anne Grey, had married Sir Henry Willoughby and on their deaths Suffolk had become guardian to their children. Also present, despite her recent bereavement, was Catherine, now strictly speaking the dowager duchess of Suffolk, although she was never referred to as such, but simply as 'my lady of Suffolk'. Open house was kept at Tylsey throughout the twelve days of Christmas and beyond, with lavish quantities of food and drink laid on for all the neighbourhood, plus entertainment by tumblers and jugglers and singing boys – the local talent being supplemented by the earl of Oxford's company of professional actors who performed several plays.[20]

James Haddon, needless to say, disapproved profoundly of such 'mummeries', which seemed to him to serve the devil by imitating a pagan saturnalia, and he lamented the way in which uninstructed country folk regarded it as almost a part of their religion to make merry after this unwholesome fashion 'on account of the birth of our Lord'. Although the nobility were now beginning to understand that it was not part of their duty so to conduct themselves, 'yet partly from the force of habit, and a desire not to appear stupid, and not good fellows, as they call it, but partly and principally, as I think, from their not having yet so far advanced as to be able perfectly to hate the garment spotted by the flesh . . . they have no settled intention much less any desire, to conquer and crucify themselves'.[21]

The godly Dr Haddon discoursed long-windedly on this head in a letter to Henry Bullinger, but appears to have had little or no success in persuading his own unregenerate flock to crucify themselves by giving up their accustomed Christmas revels. The party at Tylsey did not break up until 20 January, when the Suffolks went on to visit the duke's sister, Lady Audley, at nearby Walden.

It was two days after this that the king made a brief entry in his Journal: 'The Duke of Somerset had his head cut off upon Tower Hill between eight and nine o'clock in the morning.'[22] Edward's apparent lack of any human feelings on this occasion have earned him a reputation for callous cold-heartedness. Certainly there is no evidence that he ever made any attempt to save the duke, or even that he took any very particular interest in the proceedings against him, but did he perhaps derive some secret satisfaction from the knowledge that he was surely the first child king so effectively to have turned the tables on uncles?

Edward may have displayed no outward signs of distress over Somerset's death, but the duke's execution had been the scene of considerable public emotion. A large crowd of sympathisers assembled to witness his last moments, during which, unlike his brother, he behaved with impeccable dignity and Christian resignation, and after the deed was done there was a rush to dip handkerchiefs in his blood to be preserved as relics.

What Jane Grey thought about the death of the 'Good Duke' is not recorded. Possibly the Christmas festivities at Tylsey had been rather too much for her. At least John Ulmer, writing to Henry Bullinger in February, reports that she was just recovering from 'a severe and dangerous illness'. But she was still engrossed in her scholarly pursuits and was currently engaged 'in some extraordinary production, which will very soon be brought to light'.

Ulmer does not give any further details, but perhaps the 'extraordinary production' was connected with the recent discovery of 'a great treasure of most valuable books – Basil on Isaiah and the Psalms in Greek; Chrysostom on the Gospels in Greek; the whole of Proclus, the Platonists etc. etc.' – which had apparently been found in some parcels acquired for the duke of Suffolk from an Italian dealer.[23] Jane was still corresponding with Bullinger herself and with other German-Swiss doctors of the so-called Genevan or Calvinist sect, and in the spring of 1552 sent a present of a pair of gloves to Bullinger's wife. But although her enthusiasm remained as strong as ever, she had less time these days to devote to her intellectual interests. Her parents had never objected to them – they were fashionable and therefore desirable. All the same, now that Jane was growing up they expected her to take her place in society and not spend all her time immured in study. Learning and piety were all very well in their place, but the Suffolks had certainly not given up their hopes of exploiting their daughter's dynastic potential by seeing her make a great marriage.

Sometime during that summer of her fifteenth year she went with her mother and father to stay with the Princess Mary at Newhall Boreham in Essex, Mary's favourite country house, and it was there, according to the story handed down by Protestant tradition, that Jane once again displayed the sort of fearless honesty – or offensive bigotry, according to point of view – not calculated to endear her to her more politic elders. She was, so the story goes, walking through the chapel at Newhall with Lady Wharton, the wife of one of Mary's officers and, naturally, a devout Roman Catholic. Seeing her companion curtsy to the altar, where the Host was exposed, Jane enquired guilelessly if the Lady Mary had come in. 'No,' answered Lady Wharton, 'I made my curtsy to Him that made us all.' 'Why,' said Jane, 'how can that be, when the baker made him?'[24]

This exchange was, of course, promptly reported back to Mary, who, according to John Foxe, 'never after loved the Lady Jane as she had before'. But then the argument over the Real Presence in the Eucharist – whether the bread and wine miraculously assumed the substance of Christ's body and blood at the moment of consecration, or whether they were merely the hallowed symbols of the communicant's means of redemption – lay at the very heart of the ideological conflict which divided Catholic from Protestant. In Jane Grey's world it was a fundamental point of principle for which thousands of committed men and women were ready to (and did) suffer martyrdom, and in this context her reaction to the tacit challenge offered by Anne Wharton was perfectly in character.

During the past five years the revolution begun with the schism of 1535 had taken on a new momentum. The first parliament of Edward's reign had seen an Act repealing the Henrician additions to the old treason laws, plus the medieval statute *de Haeretico Comburendo* and the Six Articles of 1539. As well as this, all restrictions on printing, reading or teaching the Scriptures were removed and a measure enabling the laity to receive communion in both kinds – that is, in both bread and wine – was passed. This session of parliament also saw the passage of an Act dissolving the chantries and religious guilds and brotherhoods. Chantries, which could perhaps be described as a form of spiritual insurance, were endowments – usually in real estate – intended to support a priest to say regular masses for the souls of the founder and others named by him, usually members of his family, in the hope of shortening the length of time they might expect to have to spend in purgatory. The king's loving subjects assembled in parliament, however, considered this 'devising and phantasing vain opinions of purgatory and masses satisfactory, to be done for them which be departed' merely served to encourage the people's ignorance 'of their very true and perfect salvation through the death of Jesus Christ'.

The chantry priests would sometimes keep a school as a sideline and it was therefore now proposed that their endowments might well be converted to 'good and godly uses, as in erecting of grammar schools to the education of youth in virtue and godliness, the further augmentation of the Universities, and better provision for the poor and needy'.[25] In fact, it appears that only a small proportion of the assets belonging to the chantries and other similar institutions which passed into the hands of the Crown in 1548 was ever put to 'good and godly uses', and most of the grammar schools which bear the king's name owe their foundation to private benefactors.

Having done away with the ancient 'superstition' of prayers for the dead and the false doctrine of purgatory, the authorities moved briskly on to overseeing the removal of images and stained glass from parish churches, particularly in London and the south-east, always the most radical areas. Popish survivals such as the lighting of candles, kissing and decking of images were already being actively discouraged if not forbidden. The familiar ceremonies associated with Candlemas, Ash Wednesday, Palm Sunday and Good Friday were discontinued, and Whitsun 1548 passed without the usual releasing of doves from the roof of St Paul's. The 1549 prayer book had abolished much of the symbolism surrounding baptism, the blessing of the ring no longer formed part of the marriage service and the traditional cycle of feast and fast days was pared down to the major festivals of Christmas, Easter and Whitsun, with only a few saints' days still allowed.

From the early 1550s the Edwardian Reformation was increasingly influenced by the arrival from Europe of men like Martin Bucer, Peter Martyr and John a Lasco, who brought with them ideas more advanced than anything yet sanctioned in England and who, by setting up their own 'stranger churches' in London, provided patterns for an ideal reformed church which did not, of course, include bishops. This was going rather too far, but the clergy were now permitted to marry, and the communion tables, already replacing altars in parish churches, were now to be 'had down into the body of the church . . . and set in the mid-aisle among the people', while the second Book of Common Prayer, introduced in 1552, completed the process of transforming the sacrifice of the mass into a communion or commemorative service. The words of the administration, which now ran 'Take and eat this in remembrance that Christ died for thee, and feed on him in thy heart by faith with thanksgiving', could no longer be interpreted, by even the most elastic conscience, as anything but an explicit denial of the Real Presence.

In London, always a forcing-house of religious radicalism, numerous tracts, ballads and broadsheets dismissing the sacrament as no more than a Jack-in-the-Box and ridiculing Mother Mass or reviling her as the whore of Babylon had been circulating freely for some time, while rude rhymes, of the kind more often written up than written down, were sure of a success in the alehouses. A good example of the genre went as follows:

> A good mistress missa
> Shall ye go from us thissa?
> Well yet I must ye kissa
> Alack, from pain I pissa.[26]

The use of the priestly vestments associated with the celebration of mass was now forbidden, only a surplice being required, and even the act of kneeling to receive the sacrament had become hedged about with anxious denials that any form of adoration was intended.

This revised and simplified form of service also, of course, provided the government with all the excuse it needed for confiscating the vestments, plate and other valuables that were now regarded as popish and undesirable and that could be converted into urgently needed cash. In the spring of 1553, therefore, Commissions were sent round the country with instructions to have inventories made of all the church goods remaining in cathedrals and parish churches:

> That is to say, all the jewels of gold and silver, as crosses, candlesticks, censors, chalices, and all other jewels of gold and silver and ready money, which should be delivered to the master of the King's jewels in the Tower of London, and all copes and vestments of cloth of gold, cloth of tissue and cloth of silver, to be delivered to the master of the King's wardrobe in London. . . . Reserved to every cathedral and parish church a chalice or cup, or more, with tablecloths for the communion board, at the discretion of the Commissioners.[27]

In May 1551 the retiring Venetian ambassador wrote scathingly of the inconstancy of the English in matters of religion, 'for today they do one thing and tomorrow another'. Daniel Barbaro believed that there was still a good deal of dissatisfaction with the new creed, 'as shown by the insurrection of '49' and thought that if these dissidents had a leader, they might well rise again. 'On the other hand', he went on, 'the Londoners are more inclined to obedience, because they are nearer the Court. In short, the English err in their religion, and in their opinions about the faith, the ceremonies of the Church, and obedience to the Pope.' The blame for all these evils in Barbaro's opinion, should be laid at the door of Henry VIII and he proceeded to favour the Doge and Senate with a potted history of the late king's remarkable matrimonial marathon. 'In this confusion of wives, so many noblemen and great personages were beheaded, so much church plunder committed, and so many acts of disobedience perpetrated, that it may be said that all that ensued and is still going on (which to say the truth is horrible and unheard of) all, I say, is the penalty of that first sin.' Barbaro reported that 'detestation of the Pope is now so confirmed that no one, either of the new or old religion, can bear to hear him mentioned; and indeed in the litanies which they sing in church they say in English, "From the deceit and tyranny of the Bishop of Rome, Lord deliver us."' Altars, images, holy water, incense and other Roman ceremonies had disappeared and the whitewashed walls of the churches were now decorated only with 'certain Scriptural sayings.'[28]

The effect of these latest innovations was to bring the English Church still further into line with the austere Genevan or Calvinist model so admired by Jane Grey and her mentors; the Forty-two Articles of Religion published early in 1553 not only rejected transubstantiation and purgatory but embraced the Calvinistic doctrines of predestination and justification by faith alone. Whether or not this trend was maintained, however, obviously depended heavily on the king who, if he survived, would soon now be casting off the tutelage of his Council.

If he survived. . . . It was neither wise nor tactful to say such things aloud, but those with long memories must surely at times have recalled the unfortunate mortality record among young Tudor males when looking at their present king. There could still have been old men alive who would remember the death at Ludlow half a century before of the fifteen-year-old Arthur, prince of Wales. Edward's bastard half-brother Henry Fitzroy had died at seventeen and his cousin Henry Brandon at twelve – not to mention all the boy babies who had died in their cradles. Nor was Edward himself the big, strong-looking child his father had been. His fair colouring and slender physique promoted an appearance of fragility which encouraged the emissaries of those Catholic powers alarmed by evidence of his increasingly belligerent Protestantism to drop hopeful hints in their dispatches that the king of England was not likely to live long.

All the same, at fourteen Edward seemed healthy enough. The legend of the pale, consumptive little boy confined for long hours in a stuffy schoolroom dies very hard but in fact, apart from a malarial-type fever contracted when he was four years old, he seems never to have suffered even a day's illness during childhood. His timetable had always included provision for outdoor exercise and training in the sports and pastimes proper for kings and as he grew into his teens he would spend every spare moment on the tennis court, in the tiltyard or shooting at the butts. The Spanish ambassador reported that the king was beginning to exercise himself in the use of arms and enjoyed it heartily. The French ambassador complimented him on the dexterity of his sword-play, declaring that his majesty had 'borne himself right well', and receiving the modest reply from Edward that it was a small beginning, but as time passed he hoped to do his duty better.

Edward had also by this time begun to do his duty in other ways. On 14 August 1551 he had recorded in his Journal that it was 'appointed that I should come to, and sit at Council when great matters were in debating, or when I would',[29] and shortly afterwards the Emperor's ambassador reported that the king was now usually present at Council meetings 'especially when state business is being transacted'. Informed observers, though, were in no doubt as to where the real power still lay and it was noted that Northumberland's relationship with Edward was far closer than ever Somerset's had been. According to one French account, 'whenever there was something of importance that he [Northumberland] wanted done or spoken by the king without anyone knowing that it came from him, he would come secretly at night into the prince's chamber after everyone was abed. . . . The next morning this young prince would come to his council and, as if they came from himself, advocate certain matters – at which everyone marvelled, thinking they were his own ideas.'[30] John Dudley would listen deferentially to the royal opinion, while being careful to ensure that his own viewpoint should always be uppermost in Edward's mind before he slept.

At the same time it was an important part of his strategy to bring Edward forward and introduce him to the more glamorous aspects of kingship and generally ensure that he was kept happy and entertained. A true Tudor, the king thoroughly appreciated the treats and attentions being showered on him. He was still keeping regular study hours, but under Northumberland's tactful guidance his horizons were widening every day and he gave every sign of enjoying every minute of the experience.

Then in March 1552 Edward went down with a high temperature and a rash. He himself later recorded that 'I fell sick of the measles and the smallpox', but this would surely have been a lethal combination and the illness was more likely to have been an attack of measles or possibly chickenpox. He seemed to make a good recovery and was well enough to attend a St George's Day service at Westminster Abbey, wearing his Garter robes. At the end of April the court moved out to Greenwich, where the king reviewed his men-at-arms on Blackheath and ran at the ring with the lords and knights in his company. On 27 June, apparently in his usual health and spirits, he left for Hampton Court on the first stage of an ambitious progress through the south and west which took him to Portsmouth by way of Guildford, Petworth, Cowdray Park, Chichester and Bishop's Waltham. From there he went on to the Earl of Southampton's house at Tichfield and then to Southampton, Beaulieu, Christchurch and Salisbury, where he stayed with the earl of Pembroke at Wilton. The return journey was made by way of

Winchester, Basing, Newbury, Reading and Windsor, reaching Hampton Court again on 28 September.

The progress had been a triumphant personal success for the king, who had never travelled so far afield before, but the programme had been an exhausting one and people noticed that he looked pale and thin. That unlucky bout of measles, coming as it did just at the most dangerous age for Tudor boys and followed by a strenuous summer, had fatally weakened him so that by the time he got back to Westminster, two days before his fifteenth birthday, it seems highly probable that tuberculosis was already established. Girolamo Cardano, the eminent Italian physician and mathematician, had several conversations with Edward during October and was impressed by 'the excellent wit and forwardness that appeared in him' and thought him 'a boy of wondrous hope' – but at the same time he could see 'the mark in his face of death that was to come too soon'.[31]

On 30 November Edward stopped writing in his Journal. Christmas was kept at Greenwich, where a more than usually elaborate round of festivities had been arranged, possibly to distract attention from the worrying fact that the king was now far from well. When Mary came up to London early in February he was running a fever and it was three days before he was able to see her, but the Emperor's ambassador reported that the princess was received with noticeably more attention and courtesy than on previous occasions. A party of 100 gentlemen of the royal household, headed by Northumberland's eldest son, had gone out 'some way from the town to meet her' and all the great ladies, headed by the duchesses of Suffolk and Northumberland, escorted her as she rode from her house in Clerkenwell through Fleet Street to Westminster, where 'the Duke of Northumberland and the members of the Council went to receive her even to the outer gate of the palace, and did duty and obeisance to her as if she had been Queen of England'.[32] No one had yet admitted that there was anything seriously the matter with the king, but the significance of the new respect being shown to his heir was unmistakable. Edward was still in bed and Mary sat beside him while they chatted amicably about safe subjects, 'making no mention of matters of religion'.

Edward stayed in his room for the rest of the month and seemed, wrote the Imperial ambassador, 'to be sensitive to the slightest indisposition or change, partly at any rate because his right shoulder is lower than his left and he suffers a good deal when the fever is upon him, especially from a difficulty in drawing his breath, which is due to the compression of the organs on the right side. It is an important matter for consideration', continued Jehan de Scheyfve, 'especially as the illness is increasing from day to day, and the doctors have now openly declared to the Council . . . that the king's life is threatened, and if any serious malady were to supervene he would not be able to hold out long against it.'[33] However, Edward rallied temporarily in March and was able to open the second parliament of his reign, although the Lords and Commons had to go to him and a much-curtailed ceremony took place within the precincts of the palace. He stayed at Westminster over Easter, still suffering from catarrh and a cough, and on 11 April was moved back to Greenwich, always his favourite residence. De Scheyfve reported on the 28th that he was no better and had only shown himself once, in the gardens, the day after his arrival. The ambassador had heard 'from a trustworthy source' that the king was becoming steadily weaker. 'The matter he ejects from his mouth is sometimes coloured a greenish yellow and black, sometimes pink, like the colour of blood.'[34] On 12 May de Scheyfve had another gruesome bulletin for the Emperor:

The physicians are now all agreed that he is suffering from a suppurating tumour on the lung, or that at least his lung is attacked. He is beginning to break out in ulcers; he is vexed by a harsh, continuous cough, his body is dry and burning, his belly is swollen, he has a slow fever upon him that never leaves him.[35]

The government was still making every effort to conceal the gravity of the king's condition from the public but although several people were imprisoned and 'set upon the pillorie' for uttering 'most false and untrue reports touching the king's majesty's life', it was impossible to stop the rumours spreading and as spring turned into summer the atmosphere in the city was thick with speculation and alarm.

# FOUR

## JANE THE QUENE

Today I saw Lady Jane Grey walking in a grand
procession to the Tower. She is now called Queen, but is
not popular, for the hearts of the people are with Mary,
the Spanish Queen's daughter. . . . This lady is very
heretical and has never heard Mass.

Baptista Spinola, 10 July 1553

On 10 May 1553 three ships of the Company of Merchant
Venturers, led by Hugh Willoughby in the *Bona Esperanza*
and Richard Chancellor in the *Edward Bonaventure*, set
out from the Port of London on a voyage of discovery
to Muscovy and 'unknown parts of the North Seas'.
The fleet dropped downstream as far as Deptford and on
the following day sailed past Greenwich, discharging their
ordnance and shooting off their pieces in salute. They
were watched by the king from a window of the palace,
but this would be the last time that Edward was glimpsed
by anyone outside the court and the common people who
had flocked together, 'standing very thick upon the shore',
were beginning to whisper that the king was dying, poisoned
perhaps by the duke of Northumberland who planned to
seize the throne for himself.

Everyone knew that the duke's power would end with
Edward's death and few people believed that he would give
up without a struggle, but Northumberland himself appears
to have been gripped by a curious lethargy during the early

months of 1553. He was no longer a young man, fifty on his last birthday, and his health was poor. He seemed tired, depressed and out of sorts, and in a letter to a trusted underling, William Cecil, dated 3 January, spoke of his careful heart and weary body, and of his desire to escape from 'the multitude of cravers' who daily hung about his gate clamouring for money and favours. What comfort was there for him, he asked mournfully, after his long travail and troublesome life, 'and towards the end of my days?' He had always served the king faithfully and now he wanted only to seek relief from his burdens. What, after all, should he wish any longer in this life, that had seen such frailty in it?[1] But there could be no honourable retirement for a man in John Dudley's place – having once mounted the tiger of ambition there was no way to go but on, for the sake of his family if for no other reason, and John Dudley was nothing if not a devoted husband and father.

It is impossible to be certain when he finally came to terms with the fact that the king was dying, although the inference is that he clung to a desperate hope of his recovery for far longer than was reasonable. As late as 7 May he was telling Cecil of 'the joyful comfort which our physician hath this two or three mornings revived my spirit with, all which is that our sovereign lord doth begin very joyfully to amend, they having no doubt of the short recovery of his highness'.[2]

Whether or not the duke really believed the doctors, he was by this time beginning to weigh his options. These were limited. If the provisions of Henry VIII's will were followed, Mary would succeed, and at least up until the end of April Northumberland was keeping her regularly informed about the state of her brother's health and, according to de Scheyfve, had recently sent her a present of a blazon of her full arms as princess of England, which she had not borne since the days of the divorce. 'This', wrote the ambassador, 'all seems to point to his desire to conciliate the said Lady and earn her favour, and to show that he does not aspire to the crown, as I said in my preceding letters.'[3] Nevertheless, if Mary were to become queen, the best Northumberland could hope for must be total political extinction; the worst (and more likely), bodily extinction at the hands of the public executioner – he had made too many bitter enemies among the Catholics and other right-wingers who would surround her.

If Mary could somehow be excluded, there was always Elizabeth, now in her twentieth year, still unmarried and uncommitted except, perhaps, to the more moderate Protestant faction. Jehan de Scheyfve thought at one time that the duke was planning to use her as his instrument, either by marrying her to his eldest son, after first causing him to divorce his wife, 'or else that he might find it expedient to get rid of his own wife and marry the said Elizabeth himself'.[4] But Northumberland had no time to waste on such elaborate manoeuvres and, in any case, was well enough acquainted with Elizabeth Tudor to know that she would be nobody's cat's-paw. The princess had always been careful to keep on friendly terms with the duke, but there is absolutely nothing to suggest that she ever for a moment considered linking her fortunes with him, or indeed that he ever approached her on the subject. This left the Suffolk girls.

The previous year Northumberland had proposed his only remaining unmarried son, Guildford, as a match for the twelve-year-old Margaret Clifford, daughter of Eleanor Brandon, but this had been turned down by the young lady's father. Now, suddenly on a date around the end of April or beginning of May 1553, the betrothal was announced of Guildford and Jane Grey. Lady Jane, it seems, had also attempted to reject Guildford Dudley but had been forced to consent to the engagement 'by the urgency of her mother and the violence of her father, who compelled her to accede to his commands by blows'.[5]

The authority for this incident, which is faithfully and circumstantially retold by all Jane's biographers, comes from a contemporary though second-hand report by two Italians, one of whom, Raviglio Rosso, visited England the following year on a courtesy mission from the duke of Ferrara, while the other was Federigo Baoardo, or Badoer, ambassador from the republic of Venice resident at the court of Emperor Charles V in Brussels. The Italians, especially the Venetians, were usually well informed, but they were also great gossips and these accounts are necessarily based on gossip and hearsay – not that there is anything inherently improbable about the story if Jane really did attempt to defy her parents. Once the Suffolks had dreamt of seeing their eldest daughter become queen consort of England. Now that an unimaginably greater prize was being dangled before them, they would certainly have dealt ruthlessly with opposition.

The reason given for Jane's alleged recalcitrance was that she considered herself already contracted to Edward Seymour, earl of Hertford, an attractive and intelligent young man whose eligibility had, of course, died with his father. She is also said to have disliked Guildford Dudley, then about seventeen or eighteen years old. As the youngest of a large family and reputedly his mother's favourite, Guildford may have been a little spoilt. A handsome boy, he may also have been a little conceited – though all the Dudleys were good-looking. Apart from this, there does not seem to have been anything very serious known against him; and marriage, as Jane would have been well aware, offered the only possible avenue of escape from the tyranny of home. Her recoil was, therefore, more likely to have been caused by fear and distrust of her prospective father-in-law than by any special repugnance for her prospective husband. It was noticeable that outside his own immediate family circle most people, even his political allies, tended to fear and distrust John Dudley, duke of Northumberland.

Whatever the truth of the matter, any rebellion was

quickly suppressed. The duke and duchess of Suffolk had long since thrown in their lot with the Dudleys, and Jane's attitude towards her fiancé became outwardly correct, if unenthusiastic. Despite the convention that there should at least be some 'liking' between a betrothed couple, no one ever pretended that this was anything but an alliance cold-bloodedly arranged for the political, financial and dynastic advantage of the families concerned. (William Cecil heard later that the marchioness of Northampton, wife of Katherine Parr's brother, William, had been employed as go-between.) Arrangements for two other highly significant family alliances were also concluded at this time. Katherine Grey, now thirteen, was betrothed to Lord Herbert, the earl of Pembroke's heir, and a Dudley daughter, another Katherine, to Lord Hastings, son of the earl of Huntingdon and doubly descended from Plantagenet stock. Thus Northumberland and Suffolk hoped to secure the future support of Pembroke and Huntingdon, both influential figures on the political scene. Thus, too, the Dudleys had finally succeeded in breaking into the magic circle of royal kinship.

Jane Grey was married on Whit Sunday, 21 May, at Durham House, the duke of Northumberland's London residence, one of the great riverside mansions lying between Temple Bar and Charing Cross – the millionaires' row of Tudor London. It was, in fact, a triple wedding, creating a threefold line of defence, for Katherine Grey was married on the same day to the young Lord Herbert and Katherine Dudley to Henry Hastings. In spite of the haste with which the occasion had had to be organised, a great effort had been made to create an atmosphere of relaxed grandeur. 'For the more solemnity and splendour of this day, the master of the wardrobe had divers warrants to deliver out of the King's wardrobe much rich apparel and jewels.' These were to be delivered to the three brides, their mothers and Lord Guildford Dudley, and included 'certain parcels of tissues, and cloth of gold and silver' once, ironically enough, the property of the duke and duchess of Somerset.[6]

According to Raviglio Rosso, the festivities were attended by 'a great concourse of the principal persons of the kingdom', but there were some notable absentees. Neither of the princesses had been invited and, although it had been announced that the king would be present, Edward was now in no condition to leave his bed. Nor were either the French or the Imperial ambassadors among the guests at Durham House on that Sunday morning to see Lady Jane Grey, her hair braided with pearls, being led, literally, as a sacrifice to the altar.

This is not to say that the representatives of the two major Continental powers were not taking a close interest in the progress of events in London. On the contrary, English affairs in the first half of 1553 were of crucial importance to their masters. Throughout the sixteenth century pretty well every aspect of European politics was dominated by the struggle for supremacy between France and the Empire, between the rival houses of Valois and Hapsburg, between the Most Christian King Henri II and the Holy Roman Emperor Charles V, and it was a battle of giants. France might be the largest national monarchy, her frontiers now extended almost to the Rhine and with ambitions in northern Italy, but the Hapsburgs ruled over Spain and the Netherlands, plus the German Empire, the duchy of Milan and the kingdoms of Naples and Sicily, not to mention Spain's possessions in the New World. By comparison, England, that small offshore island, looked insignificant, and her international prestige was low. Nevertheless English friendship or, at the very least, neutrality, mattered a great deal to the Emperor. It was not merely that he had a personal interest just then – Mary Tudor was, after all, his first cousin – but by virtue of her strategic position, a hostile England – and especially a hostile England allied to France – would be perfectly placed to cut the vital sea-link between Spain and the Low Countries.

Jehan de Scheyfve, not a man of outstanding ability, had begun to suspect as early as February that some kind of conspiracy was being planned against the princess, but Charles, who was an old man now, suffering acutely from gout and with the cares of half of Europe on his shoulders, made no immediate move. The king of France, on the other hand, had appointed a new ambassador to London and Antoine de Noailles arrived at the end of April to find the king was too ill to see him. However, on 7 May he and the retiring ambassador visited Greenwich and in a private conversation the duke of Northumberland apparently asked them what they would do if they were in his shoes, whereupon they gave him such advice as they considered to be 'of favour and advantage' to their master's interests.[7] To underline French eagerness to seize their opportunity, Claude de l'Aubespine, a secretary often employed by Henri II on high-level diplomatic missions, came over for a brief visit at the end of the month. Despite the secrecy that surrounded the purpose of his visit, de Scheyfve heard that he had come to offer the king of France's services to Northumberland in the event of Edward's death. De Scheyfve was convinced by this time that the duke and his party intended 'to deprive the Lady Mary of the succession to the crown. . . . They are evidently resolved to resort to arms against her, with the excuse of religion among others.'[8] He also believed that they were expecting the French to help them.

Certainly the French had excellent reasons for wanting to prevent Mary from succeeding her brother – as the Emperor's cousin she would naturally take her country back into the Spanish Hapsburg camp – and in the early 1550s the French happened to be exceptionally well placed for intervention in English affairs. As a result of gross mishandling of Scottish relations by both the late king and the Protector Somerset, the 'Auld Alliance' between France and Scotland had been revived and refurbished to the extent that Scotland was currently being governed by Mary of Guise very much as a province of France, with a strong French military presence established on the other side of England's vulnerable land frontier.

Henri II also held a potential ace in the person of the little queen of Scotland, now a pretty and promising ten-year-old being brought up at his court as the future wife of his son and heir, the dauphin François. Mary Stuart might have been arbitrarily excluded from her place in the English succession by the terms of her great-uncle's will, but by all the commonly accepted rules of primogeniture her claim was unquestionably superior to that of her Suffolk cousins and, in the eyes of all orthodox Catholics, to that of her cousin Elizabeth who, as everyone knew, was a bastard born in the lifetime of King Henry's first wife. A case could also be made out to show that the queen of Scots' claim was superior to that of her cousin Mary Tudor, on whose legitimacy such grave doubts had been cast at the time of the Great Divorce. Their father's will regardless, the point could reasonably be made that both the Tudor sisters were still illegitimate by Act of Parliament. The situation, in short, fairly bristled with nice points of canon and constitutional law and, for the French, it was fraught with interesting possibilities – always provided, of course, that the duke of Northumberland could be encouraged, even perhaps assisted, to organise another *coup d'état.*

Although Jane Grey's marriage had signalled the first steps in opening moves to set aside the established line of succession, for some months before this Edward himself had been pondering ways and means of depriving his elder sister of her birthright. The king's motives appear to have been quite straightforwardly ideological. He had, after all, been raised in the purest Cambridge school of advanced intellectual and evangelical Protestantism and believed, just as rigidly as Mary did, that his was the only way of salvation for both himself and his people, for whose salvation he had always been taught he was personally responsible under God. Convictions of this kind naturally overrode all considerations of earthly justice and legality, and once he began to realise that he might not live to provide heirs of his own body Edward would have known that if he valued his immortal soul he must take every possible precaution to guard against the overthrow of the true religion now established in his realm.

In his famous Device for the Succession, a draft memorandum written in his own hand probably at the beginning of 1553, possibly even earlier, he had already fixed on the Suffolk line, and 'for lakke of issu of my body' bequeathed the crown to the Lady Frances's (that is, the duchess of Suffolk's) notional 'heires masles', then to the Lady Jane's 'heires masles' and so on through the family. But as his condition began to deteriorate, and the fact had to be faced that neither his aunt Frances nor any of his so regrettably female cousins were going to produce heirs male in the immediate future, the king made a simple but radical change to his Device, leaving the throne to 'the Lady Jane and her heires masles'.[9]

Why he chose to exclude his Protestant sister, to whom he was supposedly devoted, as well as his Catholic one has never been fully explained. He may have felt it would be inequitable and impractical to deprive one of the princesses and not the other; he may have feared that Elizabeth, however good her intentions, might find herself obliged to marry some Catholic prince; or he may have sensed that she would have rejected any bequest based on such an obvious injustice. The official reasons, as set out in the letters patent for the Limitation of the Crown – the Device in its final form – were that the Ladies Mary and Elizabeth were 'illegitimate and not lawfully begotten', related to the king by half-blood only and therefore not entitled to succeed him, and liable to marry foreign husbands whose control of the government would inevitably 'tend to the utter subversion of the commonwealth of this our realm'.[10]

The question of whether or not either or both of Henry VIII's daughters could properly be regarded as lawfully begotten was and remains debatable. The other grounds alleged for their exclusion from the succession were constitutionally merely frivolous and, in any case, no will, Device or letters patent issued by Edward could have any validity in law as long as the 1544 Act of Succession, 35 Henry VIII, remained on the Statute Book; nor, for that matter, could Edward, as a minor, make a valid will. But for the dying king, for the duke of Northumberland, now committed beyond the point of no return, for the king of France waiting hopefully in the wings, the legality of the scheme mattered far less than the speed and efficiency with which it could be put into effect.

It was by this time becoming only too obvious that speed was likely to be of the essence. On 17 May Edward had finally been able to see the French ambassadors, who reported him to be weak and still troubled by a cough. De Scheyfve heard that their audience had only been granted to reassure the people 'and that the doctors and physicians were persuaded to allow it for that reason'. At the end of the month he wrote that the king was wasting away daily and there was no sign or likelihood of any improvement. 'Some', he went on, 'are of the opinion that he may last two months more, but he cannot possibly live beyond that time. He cannot rest except by means of medicines and external applications; and his body has begun to swell, especially his head and feet.'[11] A fortnight later de Scheyfve was writing again to report that Edward had been attacked on 11 June 'by a violent hot fever which lasted over 24 hours' and which had recurred on the 14th, 'more violent than before'. At this point the doctors had given him up, saying that he might die at any time, 'because he is at present without the strength necessary to rid him of certain humours which, when he does succeed in ejecting them, give forth a stench. Since the 11th he has been unable to keep anything in his stomach, so he lives entirely on restoratives and obtains hardly any repose.'[12] All the same, it was essential to keep the sufferer alive for a few more weeks and it may have been at this time that, according to Edward's first biographer, the Council adopted the desperate expedient of dismissing his doctors and bringing in an unnamed 'gentlewoman' who had promised to cure him, provided 'he were committed wholly to her hand'. She proceeded to dose the wretched boy with 'restringents' which probably included arsenic and which seem to have produced a temporary rally.[13]

In order to give the Device for the Succession a cloak of respectability, it would be necessary to carry the Privy Council, the judiciary and the bishops, and consequently Sir Edward Montagu, Chief Justice of the Common Pleas, was ordered to appear at Greenwich on 12 June, bringing with him Sir John Baker, Chancellor of the Exchequer, Mr Justice Bromley, Edward Gryffyn the Attorney General, and John Gosnold the Solicitor General. They were brought into the king's presence and Edward there and then 'by his own mouth' informed them of his intentions with regard to his successor and presented them with a signed copy of his Device commanding them 'to make a book thereof accordingly with speed'.

To do them justice the lawyers, led by Edward Montagu, did their best to resist. But when they tried to point out to the lords of the Council that the king was in effect asking them to commit treason, and that any attempt to execute his Device after his death would also be treason, the duke of Northumberland stormed into the council chamber 'being in a great rage and fury . . . and called Sir Edward Montagu traitor, and further said that he would fight in his shirt with any man in that quarrel'. The lawyers were summoned to Greenwich again on the 15th when the king 'with sharp words and angry countenance' asked them why they had not 'made his book according to his commandment'.

He would listen to no legal arguments about the authority of parliament, ordering them to obey 'upon their allegiance', so that Edward Montagu, being 'in great fear as ever he was in his life before, seeing the king so earnest and sharp, and the duke so angry . . . who ruled the whole council as it pleased him' gave in and agreed to draw up the necessary documents.[14]

The Limitation of the Crown passed the Great Seal on 21 June and by the end of the month it had been endorsed, more or less reluctantly, by the Lord Chancellor, the Privy Councillors, twenty-two peers of the realm, the Lord Mayor of London, the aldermen and sheriffs of Middlesex, Surrey and Kent, the officers of the royal household, the Secretaries of State (even that super-cautious individual William Cecil had been obliged to add his signature), the judges and the bishops, headed by Thomas Cranmer. Cranmer, like Montagu, had had serious reservations and believed that if he had been allowed to see the king alone, he might have 'altered him from his purpose'. But more than anything else the compassionate archbishop wanted to see his much-loved godson die in peace, happy in the belief that he had ensured the survival of the true Protestant religion, and when he set his hand to the fatal document, he did so 'unfeignedly and without dissimulation'.[15]

He was only just in time. On 19 June de Scheyfve reported that the king's state was such that he himself had given up hope, 'and says he feels so weak that he can resist no longer, and that he is done for'.[16] Five days later the ambassador wrote he had just been told 'that the King of England's present condition is such that he cannot possibly live more than three days . . . for he has not the strength to stir, and can hardly breathe. His body no longer performs its functions, his nails and hair are dropping off, and all his person is scabby.'[17] Edward's contemporaries believed that he was suffering from the same disease that had killed his illegitimate half-brother the duke of Richmond – that is, consumption, or pulmonary tuberculosis – and later historians have followed this hypothesis. However, recent medical opinion has suggested that his illness was more likely to have been a suppurating pulmonary infection, developing into 'acute bilateral bronchopneumonia' and finally the general septicaemia which would have killed him.[18] Whatever the cause, there can be no doubt that his sufferings were terrible. His doctors had now been allowed back into the sickroom, but there was nothing they could do and the boy who had been born amid such joy and wondrous hope fifteen years and nine months ago longed only for release, which came between eight and nine o'clock on the evening of Thursday 6 July, when the last Tudor king died in the arms of his friend Henry Sidney.

The six weeks which had passed since her marriage had not been happy ones for Lady Jane Dudley and she seems to have developed such an aversion to her husband's family that even her own mother's company was preferable. Apparently she had been promised that she could continue to live at home for a time after the wedding and immediately after the ceremony she had gone back first to Suffolk House at Westminster and then to her parents' grand new suburban residence, converted from the former Carthusian monastery on the Thames at Sheen. But the duchess of Northumberland, who did not get on with the duchess of Suffolk, soon became impatient with this foolishness. She told Jane that the king was dying and that she must hold herself in readiness for a summons at any moment, because he had made her the heir to his dominions.

According to Jane's own account, this was the first she had heard of the seriousness of Edward's illness and the news, flung at her without warning, caused her the greatest agitation and alarm, but she did not take it seriously, putting it down to 'boasting' and an excuse to separate her from her mother. Being Jane, she probably said as much, for the result was a furious quarrel, with the duchess of

Northumberland accusing the duchess of Suffolk of trying to keep the newly-weds apart and insisting that, whatever happened, Jane's place was with her husband. This argument was unanswerable and Jane was forced to join Guildford at Durham House where, possibly, the marriage was consummated.

But the reluctant bride stayed only two or three nights with her in-laws. She had fallen ill – probably with some form of 'summer complaint' aggravated by nervous strain – and, with a surprising lack of logic, became convinced that the Dudleys were trying to poison her. In fact, of course, her health and well-being were vital to the Dudleys just then, and they sent her out to Chelsea, with its happy memories of Katherine Parr, to rest and recuperate. She was still there on the afternoon of 9 July when her sister-in-law, Northumberland's eldest daughter Mary Sidney, came to fetch her to go to Syon House – another former convent on the banks of the Thames which had been commandeered by the duke – in order to receive 'that which had been ordered for me by the king'. She told me, says Jane, 'with extraordinary seriousness, that it was necessary for me to go with her, which I did'.

At Syon Jane found her parents, her mother-in-law, the marquess and marchioness of Northampton, the earls of Huntingdon, Arundel and Pembroke, and the Duke of Northumberland in his capacity of Lord President of the Council. These distinguished personages greeted her with 'unwonted caresses and pleasantness' and, to her acute embarrassment, proceeded to do her 'such reverence as was not at all suitable to my state, kneeling down before me on the ground, and in many other ways, making semblance of honouring me'. Northumberland then broke the news of Edward's death, declaring 'what cause we had all to rejoice for the virtuous and praiseworthy life that he had led, as also for his very good death. Furthermore he pretended to comfort himself and the by-standers by praising much his prudence and goodness, for the very great care that he had taken of his kingdom at the very close of his life.' The exact nature of his late majesty's care was now officially disclosed to his heiress, as the duke announced the terms of the king's Device, how he had decided for good and sufficient reasons that neither of his sisters was worthy to succeed him and how – 'he being in every way able to disinherit them' – he had instead nominated his cousin Jane to follow him on to the throne of England.

It has generally been accepted that this was the first Jane knew of the deadly inheritance thrust upon her, and certainly she had taken no part in the internecine manoeuvrings of the past few months. But at the same time it is difficult to accept that this highly intelligent, highly educated young woman can really have been so unworldly as not to have grasped the underlying significance of her hastily arranged marriage; or that she had not at least guessed something of what was being planned for her. Not, of course, that prior knowledge would in any way have affected the helplessness of her position. On the contrary, Jane's nightmare lay in her awareness that she had become the prisoner of a power-hungry, unscrupulous junta, led by the man she had come to fear above all others. As she was later to call on those present to bear witness, she fell to the ground overcome by shock and distress, half fainting and weeping very bitterly, while the lords of the Council knelt before her, solemnly swearing to shed their blood in defence of her right. She managed to gasp out something about her 'insufficiency' and muttered a hasty prayer that if to succeed to the throne was indeed her duty and her right, God would help her to govern the realm to his glory. God, on that traumatic Sunday evening, looked like being her only friend.[19]

On the following day, Monday 10 July, the new queen was taken in full state down-river from Syon to Westminster. The royal party probably dined at Durham House and then entered their barges again to complete their journey to the Tower, the great fortress-palace where, according to ancient custom, all new sovereigns came to take possession at the beginning of their reigns. Jane and her entourage arrived about three o'clock in the afternoon and a Genoese merchant, Baptista Spinola, who was standing among a group of spectators waiting to see the procession disembark, took the trouble to describe her appearance in considerable detail. 'This Jane', he wrote, 'is very short and thin [all the Grey sisters were tiny – Mary, the youngest, to the point of deformity], but prettily shaped and graceful. She has small features and a well-made nose, the mouth flexible and the lips red. The eyebrows are arched and darker than her hair, which is nearly red. Her eyes are sparkling and *rosso* [hazel] in colour.' Spinola was standing so close to Jane that he noticed her complexion was good but freckled and her teeth, when she smiled, white and sharp. She had been put into chopines – shoes with a specially raised cork sole – to make her look taller and more visible and was wearing a gown of green velvet stamped with gold; while Guildford Dudley, 'a very tall strong boy with light hair', resplendent in a suit of white and silver, preened himself at her side and 'paid her much attention'.[20]

According to the Italians, some of the beholders were shocked at the sight of the duchess of Suffolk acting as her daughter's train-bearer on this occasion, and some foreigners were surprised that the duchess had not been named as her nephew's heir. This must certainly have seemed more logical to outsiders, unaware of the detailed provisions of Henry VIII's will. According to the French ambassador, the duchess herself was seriously aggrieved at having been passed over and de Noailles also states that he 'knew' the duke of Suffolk bitterly resented his wife's exclusion from her rightful place in the succession. But it had never been any part of Northumberland's plan to elevate Jane's parents to regal status and, whatever had gone on behind the scenes, in public they gave no sign of having expected it – rather it seems they were content to bask in their daughter's reflected glory. Guildford Dudley, however, was expecting a great deal of regal status.

Guildford was enjoying himself. He made no pretence of loving his wife – probably he regarded her as a tiresome little prig – but he was quite prepared to be polite to her in public in return for the golden stream of social and material benefits which would flow from her. Unfortunately these happy expectations were about to receive a severe setback. No sooner was Jane installed in the now-vanished royal apartments than she was visited by the Lord Treasurer, the old marquess of Winchester, bringing a selection of royal jewels for her inspection. He also brought the crown itself, although, as Jane was later to stress, 'it had never been demanded from him by me, or by anyone in my name'. In what was most likely an attempt to force her into committing herself beyond any possibility of retreat, Winchester urged her to try it on, to see if it became her. Jane recoiled in horror. In her eyes the crown represented the ultimate symbol of sanctified earthly power; to treat it as a plaything for boys and girls, a sort of extra-special headdress, would be tantamount to violating a sacred mystery. But Winchester failed to recognise the storm signals. She could take it without fear, he told her, adding casually that another would be made to crown her husband withal.

That was the final straw. It was perhaps only then that Jane realised 'with infinite grief and displeasure of heart' the full extent of the cynical trick which had been played on her. In spite of all their pious speeches, no one cared a snap of their fingers about fulfilling the dead king's wishes, about maintaining the gospel and the true Protestant religion, or even whether the crown was rightfully hers. The plot was simply to use her and her royal blood to raise a plebeian Dudley to a throne to which he had no shadow of right, so that his father could continue to rule. Jane possessed her full share of Tudor family pride and now that pride was outraged. Small, stubborn, terrified and furious, she laid back her ears and dug in her heels. She would make her husband a duke but never, never would she agree to make him king. In any case, she pointed out coldly, nothing could be done without the consent of parliament.

This precipitated another full-scale family row. Guildford rushed away to fetch his mother and together they launched an all-out assault on their victim – he whining that he didn't want to be a duke, he wanted to be king; she scolding like a fishwife. At last, finding Jane immovable, they stormed out of her presence, the duchess of Northumberland swearing that her precious son should not stay another moment with his unnatural and ungrateful wife but would return immediately to Syon. Jane watched them go and then summoned the earls of Arundel and Pembroke. Little though she cared for Guildford's company, she had no intention of allowing him to put such a public slight on her, and she instructed Arundel and Pembroke to prevent him from leaving. Their positions were now, somewhat ironically, reversed. Whether Guildford shared her bed or not, his place was at her side and there he must stay. Guildford sulked but did as he was told, 'and thus' Jane was to write, 'I was compelled to act as a woman who is obliged to live on good terms with her husband; nevertheless I was not only deluded by the duke and the council, but maltreated by my husband and his mother'.[21]

While these domestic battles were raging inside the Tower, the sheriff of London, with three heralds, a trumpeter and an escort of the guard, had made his way to the Cross in Cheapside to proclaim Jane, the duke of Suffolk's daughter, as the new queen of England. But, noted the *Greyfriars Chronicle* ominously, 'few or none said God save her'. Gilbert Pot, or Potter, tapster at the St John's Head tavern within Ludgate, went so far as to declare that 'the Lady Mary had the better title' and was promptly arrested and set in the pillory for his pains.[22]

On paper John Dudley's position looked to be unassailable. The reign of his daughter-in-law and puppet queen had begun; he controlled the capital, the Tower with its armoury, the treasury and the navy, while the lords of the Council, all apparently hypnotised by his powerful personality, waited meekly to do his bidding. It seemed, too, that he could rely on the enthusiastic support of the French: Antoine de Noailles was already referring to Guildford Dudley as 'the new king'. His only adversary was a frail, sickly woman of thirty-seven, without money, influence, professional advice or organised support of any kind. No informed observer of the political scene believed that Mary Tudor stood a chance of enforcing her claim against a man like Northumberland – least of all, it appeared, her only friend and ally the Holy Roman Emperor.

News of French intervention in the developing crisis in England had finally prodded Charles into action and on 23 June three special envoys had been dispatched from Brussels. Their instructions made it clear that their prime objective was to take such steps as they considered necessary 'to defeat the machinations of the French and keep them out of England'. Of course they were to do what they could to assist and protect Mary, but it was plain that their only weapons would be diplomacy and persuasion, and that, in the last resort, an English alliance was more important to the Emperor than his cousin's right to her throne.[23]

The Imperial ambassadors arrived in London on 6 July and although the king's death was being kept a close secret – or as close as it was possible to keep any secret in a royal household – they quickly picked up the news from an informant in the palace. On the following day they sent off their first report, taking a thoroughly gloomy view of the situation. All the forces of the country, they wrote, were in the hands of the duke, 'and my Lady [Mary] has no hope of raising enough men to face him, nor of assisting those who may espouse her cause. . . . The hope that my Lady builds upon English supporters of her claim is vain, because of religion; and to proclaim herself without hope of (immediate) success would only jeopardise those chances that remain to her of coming to the throne.' The ambassadors were of the opinion that 'the actual possession of power was a matter of great importance, especially among barbarians like the English' – even as they wrote they received information that one of Northumberland's sons had already set out with 300 horse and they believed that his orders were to seize the Lady Mary.[24]

And yet, even as they wrote, control was beginning to slip out of Northumberland's hands. In spite of appearances, the duke knew well enough how narrow his power base actually was. Certainly he harboured no illusions about the loyalty of his confederates if the going were to get rough. Survival now would depend on swift, bloodless success and that in turn depended on the swift and inconspicuous elimination of all opposition. On or about 4 July Mary and Elizabeth were both sent letters summoning them to see the king. Elizabeth made no move, prudently taking to her bed with a convenient illness. Mary, who had been waiting out the past few months in 'sore perplexity' and increasing fear for the future, was then at the old nursery palace at Hunsdon in Hertfordshire and set out, albeit hesitantly, on the journey to Greenwich. She had not gone far, no further than Hoddesdon on the London road, before a warning reached her that the summons was a trap. (Nicholas Throckmorton later claimed the credit for having dispatched the princess's goldsmith on this vital errand.) Reacting with uncharacteristic decisiveness, she at once turned round and, accompanied by no more than half a dozen trusted household servants, made for Kenninghall, the Howard family stronghold in Norfolk. She had some good friends in East Anglia and there, if the worst came to the worst, she would be within reach of the coast and escape to the Spanish Netherlands.

Meanwhile in London, the new regime was doing all the expectable things. The ports had been closed and the Lord Treasurer Winchester, the earl of Shrewsbury, the marquess of Northampton, and the Lord Admiral Lord Clinton came to 'inspect' the Tower, key fortress of the realm. Clinton was installed as Constable and the garrison could be seen hauling out the heavy guns and mounting them ready for use. On Saturday 8 July the Lord Mayor and a delegation of aldermen and other leaders of the mercantile community were called to the court to be told of the king's death and his provisions for the succession, 'to the which they were sworn and charged to keep it secret'.[25]

Northumberland would naturally have preferred to go on keeping it secret until such time as he had got his hands on either or both of the rival claimants, but when it became apparent that Mary had, temporarily at least, slipped through his fingers, he could wait no longer and on Sunday the 9th the bishop of London, preaching at Paul's Cross, referred to both princesses explicitly as bastards, but fulminated especially against Mary as a stiff papist who, if she became queen, would overturn the true religion and betray the country to a foreign power.[26] By the following day Jane's proclamation had been printed in black letter by Richard Grafton, ready to be posted up in the city of London and in church porches and market crosses up and down the land. A letter had also been drafted in the duke's own hand to be distributed to the Lords Lieutenant of the counties under Jane's signature, announcing her entry into her Tower of London 'as rightful queen of this realm' and requiring her 'right trusty and well beloved' councillors to endeavour to the utmost of their power 'not only to defend our just title, but also to assist us . . . to disturb, repel and resist the feigned and untrue claim of the Lady Mary, bastard daughter to our great uncle Henry th' Eight, of famous memory'.[27]

But on that same eventful Monday a letter had been delivered to the lords of the Council from the Lady Mary herself, now in temporary sanctuary at Kenninghall, expressing dignified surprise that they had failed to inform her of 'so weighty a matter' as her brother's death and commanding them upon their allegiance forthwith to cause *her* right and title to the crown and government of the realm to be proclaimed in her city of London.[28] Their lordships, it seems, were 'greatly astonished and troubled' by the unwelcome news that Mary was still at large and showing fight and, so they heard at the Imperial embassy, the duchesses of Suffolk and Northumberland both shed tears of mortification. At the Imperial embassy, though, they were still confidently expecting the worst. They had not ventured to make direct contact with Mary, nor to answer her anguished appeals for help, and could only deplore her stubborn refusal to accept the inevitability of defeat, expecting at any moment to hear that she had been seized and 'subjected to evil treatment, if the news that are coming in from all quarters are true'.[29]

Inside the Tower an air of carefully studied calm prevailed. The Council wrote sternly back to Mary, reminding her of the sundry Acts of Parliament by which she was 'justly made illegitimate and uninheritable to the Crown Imperial of this realm' and requiring her to cease by any pretence to vex and molest the loyal subjects of 'our Sovereign Lady Queen Jane'. If she showed herself quiet and obedient as she ought, then the lords would be glad to do her any service 'that we with duty may'; if not, they indicated, she would be sorry.[30] The Council also dispatched a messenger to Brussels with a letter authorising him to inform the Emperor of King Edward's death and another letter, over the sign manual of 'Jane the Quene', instructing Sir Philip Hoby to continue in his post of resident ambassador at the Imperial court, while young Guildford Dudley amused himself by drafting a document giving Sir Philip full powers to deal in *his* affairs. There was talk of a coronation in two weeks' time and a requisition had been sent to the Master of the Wardrobe for twenty yards of velvet, twenty-five ells of fine Holland, or linen cloth, and thirty-three ells of coarser material to make lining for robes. More boxes of jewels had now been delivered to the Tower, but unfortunately they seem mostly to have contained a miscellany of odds and ends such as every household accumulates, including, among other things, a toothpick in the shape of a fish, an assortment of buttons, semi-precious stones and trinkets, a number of 'purse-hangers of silver and gilt', two billaments (the jewelled borders worn on ladies' hoods), and a clock of damascened work made in the shape of a book. There was a prayer book, a leather purse, some coins, even a pair of silver 'twitchers' or tweezers.[31]

So far the determination to present a confident face to the outside world was holding. Antoine de Noailles, who had seen the Council on 7 July and generously offered his master's help should need arise, remained optimistic; in contrast, the Imperial ambassadors were still so nervous that for several days they scarcely dared to leave de Scheyfve's house and then only went out for a brief airing in the company of a few Spanish merchants – 'To help themselves to show a little spirit,' wrote de Noailles unkindly.[32] All the same, it was the Imperialists who detected the first signs of a crack in the façade when, on Wednesday 12 July, they received a visit from Lord Cobham and Sir John Mason on behalf of Northumberland.

Of the three special envoys sent by Charles, it was Simon Renard, a native of the Franche Comté and a brilliant, hard-working, subtle career diplomat, who had taken the lead. When Cobham and Mason began in a hectoring manner, telling them that their credentials were no longer valid now that Edward was dead, forbidding them to attempt to communicate with Mary and threatening them with England's 'barbarous laws' if they gave any cause for suspicion, it was Renard who replied, tactfully assuring the councillors of the Emperor's goodwill and urging them rather to welcome the advances of old friends than seek new alliances with those who had always been their enemies. The French, he pointed out, had a vested interest in stirring up trouble, their object being 'to seek to gain a foothold in England for their own ends and to the advantage of the Queen of Scotland and that of her affianced spouse, the Dauphin of France'. When the Emperor heard that his cousin had been declared a bastard and of 'the violence that was publicly said to be intended against her person', he would naturally conclude that French intrigues had prevailed and that the rights long recognised by the international community as belonging to Mary had been snatched away to gain the crown for the queen of Scots, under colour of conferring it upon the duke of Suffolk's daughter. Renard ended by saying that if the Council really regarded their commission as having expired, then he and his colleagues must ask to be supplied with an escort so that they might return to Brussels, and did this mean that de Scheyfve, the resident ambassador, was no longer welcome either?

Renard and the others had the satisfaction of seeing Cobham and Mason reduced to embarrassed silence. Nor did they miss the shifty exchange of glances between the two men as they began to back-pedal, murmuring that of course it had been a mistake to say the ambassadors' commission had expired and hoping their excellencies would not feel obliged to ask for their passports until the Council had been able to consider the position further. 'So,' wrote Renard, 'they left us in suspense, waiting to see what they would say or do.'[33]

Although the anxiously waiting envoys had heard unconfirmed reports that Northumberland's son Robert had been defeated by Mary's followers and also believed that there were 'many people in the realm who love the Lady Mary and hate the duke and his children, and would gladly help her if they could', they were still in

daily expectation of hearing that she had fallen into the
hands of her enemies. But on that same Wednesday, 12
July, some very disquieting news had reached the Council
of the support now rallying to her. The earl of Bath, the
earl of Sussex and his son, Sir Thomas Wharton, Sir
John Mordaunt, Sir William Drury and Sir John Shelton,
together with substantial families like the Bedingfields,
Bacons, Jerninghams and Cornwallises were already with
her, or on their way. Any hope of being able to present a
grumbling but acquiescent nation with a *fait accompli* had
now vanished. Instead a full-scale expedition would have to
be mounted to 'fetch in the Lady Mary' and the issue would
have to be decided on the field of battle.

There was clearly no time to be lost and a muster was
hurriedly ordered in Tothill Fields, the unusually high
rate of pay offered, ten pence a day, being a measure of
the regime's concern. It had been intended to put the
duke of Suffolk in command of the army, but when this
information was conveyed to Queen Jane on the evening of
12 July she promptly burst into tears and begged that her
father 'might tarry at home in her company'. Jane seems
to have forgotten that she had once thought it hell to be in
her parents' company – but she hadn't known the Dudley
family then.

The assembled lords of the Council gazed thoughtfully
at their weeping sovereign lady and then at one another,
an idea forming (or, more likely, already formed) in
their collective mind. This idea they propounded to the
duke of Northumberland. It would surely be better, they
suggested, if he took command himself. No other man was
so well fitted for the task, especially since he had already
successfully suppressed one rebellion in East Anglia and
was therefore so feared in those parts that no one would
dare to offer him resistance. Besides, was he not 'the best
man of war in the realm?' Then there was the matter of
the queen's distress, and the fact that she would 'in no

wise grant that her father should take it on him'. So it was really up to the duke, remarked someone, a note of steel suddenly audible beneath the flattery and subservience; it was up to the duke to 'remedy the matter'. And the duke gave way. 'Since ye think it good,' he said, 'I and mine will go, not doubting your fidelity to the queen's majesty which I leave in your custody.'[34]

The fidelity of his associates to anything but their own best interests was, of course, highly doubtful, and it was a lively fear of what they might do as soon as his back was turned that lay behind John Dudley's reluctance to take the field himself. He was well aware that he was being manoeuvred into the role of possible scapegoat, but there was no turning back now. Even as they sat talking round the council table in the summer dusk the sound of heavy wagons laden with weapons and supplies – 'great guns and small, bows, bills, spears, morris-pikes, harness [armour], arrows, gunpowder and victuals, money, tents and all manner of ordnance' – could be heard rattling eastward through the city streets 'for a great army toward Cambridge'.[35] The decision taken, Northumberland and the others waited on the Lady Jane to tell her of their conclusion, 'who humbly thanked the duke for reserving her father at home and beseeched him to use his diligence'. 'I will do what in me lies,' he answered, looking down at the thin, redheaded slip of a girl, to whom he was now bound by the unbreakable kinship of mutual destruction.[36]

Preparations continued throughout the next day. Early in the morning the duke called for his personal armour and saw it made ready, before appointing his own retinue to meet him at Durham Place. Then, his arrangements made, he returned to the Tower to address the assembled Council for the last time. After urging that reinforcements should be sent without fail to join him at Newmarket, he made a last attempt to assert the old dominant force of his personality. He and his companions, he said, were going forth to adventure their bodies and lives 'amongst the bloody strokes and cruel assaults' of the enemy, trusting themselves and their wives and children at home to the faith and truth of those they left behind. If anyone present were planning to violate that trust and 'to leave us your friends in the briars and betray us', let them remember that treachery could be a two-handed game. Let them also reflect on God's vengeance and the sacred oath of allegiance they had taken 'to this virtuous lady the Queen's highness, who by your and our enticement is rather of force placed therein than by her own seeking and request'. There was, too, the matter of God's cause. The fear of papistry's re-entry had, after all, been the original ground on which everyone had agreed and 'even at the first motion granted your goodwills and assents thereto, as by your hands' writing evidently appeareth'. John Dudley could say no more but in this troublesome time to wish his hearers 'to use constant hearts, abandoning all malice, envy and private affections . . . and this I pray you,' he ended, 'wish me no worse speed in his journey than ye would have to yourselves'.

'My lord,' said someone – it may have been Winchester, the oldest of the peers – 'if ye mistrust any of us in this matter, your grace is far deceived; for which of us can wipe his hands clean thereof?' While they were still talking the servants had come in with the first course of dinner and were laying the table, but Winchester (if it were he) went on: 'If we should shrink from you as one that were culpable, which of us can excuse himself as guiltless? Therein your doubt is too far cast.' 'I pray God it be so,' answered Northumberland abruptly. 'Let us go to dinner.'

After the lords had eaten, the duke went to take his formal leave of the queen and receive from her his signed and sealed commission as Lieutenant of her army. Coming out through the council chamber he encountered the earl of Arundel, 'who prayed God be with his grace; saying he was very sorry it was not his chance to go with him and bear him company, in whose presence he could find it in his

119

heart to spend his blood, even at his foot'.[37] Henry FitzAlan did not add that he, together with the earls of Shrewsbury and Pembroke, the Lord Privy Seal John Russell, Lord Cobham, John Mason and Secretary William Petre, would be having a private meeting with the Imperial ambassadors later that very day. But then nor was Northumberland advertising the fact that he had just dispatched his cousin Henry Dudley on an urgent mission to the king of France, offering, so it is said, to trade Ireland and Calais in exchange for immediate French military assistance.

The situation was still highly volatile and, in an atmosphere thick with suspicion and distrust, rumour and counter-rumour bred and multiplied. Reports were now coming in that the gentry were proclaiming Queen Mary in Buckinghamshire, but the Emperor's ambassadors, in a dispatch dated 14 July, continued to predict the likelihood of her imminent defeat, for the duke was raising men wherever he could and was strong on land and at sea. 'So, as far as we can see,' they went on, 'none of the people who are secretly attached to the Lady Mary can or dare declare for her or rise, unless they hear that she is being supported by your Majesty.' Meanwhile, Mary herself, who had now retreated to Framlingham Castle, a stronger place than Kenninghall and nearer the coast, had sent a courier with a verbal message that 'she saw destruction hanging over her' unless the Emperor helped her quickly.[38]

Northumberland had succeeded in raising an army of around 3,000 horse and foot, and early on the morning of Friday 14 July he rode out from Durham Place, turning east down the Strand towards the Cambridge road and 'towards the Lady Mary's grace to destroy her grace'. But as his cavalcade passed through the village of Shoreditch, where the way was lined with silent, staring crowds, the duke turned to Lord Grey of Wilton, who was riding alongside him and observed grimly: 'The people press to see us, but not one sayeth God speed us.'[39]

During the next few days the faces of those left cooped up in the Tower grew steadily longer as word arrived that Mary had been proclaimed in Norwich and that the town, one of the largest and richest in the country, was sending her men and supplies. Colchester had also declared for her, and in places as far apart as Devon and Oxfordshire the leaders of the local community were following suit. More and more gentlemen 'with their powers' (that is, their tenantry and dependants) were voting with their feet by joining the growing camp at Framlingham, while the noblemen's tenants showed ominous signs of refusing to serve their lords against Queen Mary, and the duke's own army was being plagued by internal dissension and desertion.

Then came a really shattering piece of news. The crews of the six royal ships sent to watch the port of Yarmouth and cut off Mary's escape to the Low Countries had gone over to her in a body, taking their captains and their heavy guns with them. 'After once the submission of the ships was known in the Tower,' wrote an eye-witness, 'each man then began to pluck in his horns' – and when Northumberland wrote querulously from his command post in the old Brandon territory of Bury St Edmunds, complaining about the non-arrival of his promised and much-needed reinforcements, he received 'but a slender answer'.[40] This was hardly surprising, since from the moment of the navy's defection it had been a question not of whether but of when the lords of the Council would follow the sailors' example. Already certain individuals, notably the earl of Pembroke and Thomas Cheyne, Lord Warden of the Cinque Ports, were looking for an excuse to go out and 'consult' in London, and on the 16th there was an alarm at about seven o'clock in the evening when 'the gates of the Tower upon a sudden was shut, and the keys carried up to Queen Jane'. It was given out that a seal had gone missing, but the author of *The Chronicle of Queen Jane* believed the truth of the matter was that her highness suspected the Lord Treasurer of some evil intent. Old Winchester had apparently sneaked out to his own house and had to be fetched back at midnight.[41] The other lords were not risking any one of their number stealing a march at this stage.

Inside the Tower they were still going through the motions. Jane was still solemnly signing letters addressed to the sheriffs and justices of the peace requiring them to take steps to suppress the 'rebellion' of the Lady Mary, but there was of course no question of her being able to stem the tide; she had neither the experience nor the authority, nor did her father command the respect of his peers. By 18 July the earls of Arundel, Bedford, Pembroke, Shrewsbury and Worcester, Lords Paget and Cobham and about half a dozen others were ready to move, leaving the Tower *en masse* on the not very convincing excuse of having urgent matters to discuss with the French ambassador. Instead, they assembled for a conference at Baynard's Castle, Pembroke's house on the riverbank below Ludgate Hill, and the following afternoon it was the Imperial embassy which received a visit from the earl of Shrewsbury and Sir John Mason. They came to explain to the Emperor's representatives how reluctant they and their fellow councillors had been to subscribe to King Edward's Device for the Succession, but really they had had no choice, for they had been so bullied by Northumberland and treated almost as if they were prisoners. Of course they had always believed in their hearts that Mary was the rightful queen and they were going to proclaim her in London that very day.[42]

And so they did, between five and six o'clock in the evening of Wednesday 19 July at the Cross in Cheapside amid scenes of wild popular rejoicing. People with money in their pockets flung it out of windows into the cheering, yelling crowds below. The earl of Pembroke was seen to throw a whole capful of gold angels and no doubt regarded it as a good investment. Sober citizens tore off their gowns and capered in the streets like children. Church bells rang a joyful peal from a forest of steeples and *Te Deum* was sung at St Paul's. Bonfires blazed up on every corner and all that night the people of London sang and danced and feasted, drinking the health of the rightful queen, God bless her! and destruction to her enemies. All observers agreed that such scenes of rejoicing had seldom if ever been known and 'what with shouting and crying of the people, and ringing of the bells, there could no one hear almost what another said, besides banqueting and singing in the street for joy'.[43]

# FIVE

# JANA NON REGINA

Although my fault be great, and I confess it to be so, nevertheless I am charged and esteemed guilty more than I have deserved. For whereas I might take upon me that of which I was not worthy, yet no one can ever say either that I sought it as my own, or that I was pleased with it.

Jane Grey

Faint echoes of the rejoicing in the city could be heard even inside the Tower, where, so it is said, the duke of Suffolk presently came to break the news to his daughter as she sat at supper, and with his own hands helped to tear down the cloth of estate above her head. Then, ordering his men to leave their weapons behind, he went out on to Tower Hill, saying helplessly, 'I am but one man,' and proclaimed the Lady Mary's grace to be queen of England, before scuttling away to his house at Sheen.[1] Jane was left alone in the stripped and silent rooms to listen to the distant clamour of the bells. For her there would be no going home. When Lady Throckmorton, one of the ladies of the household who had gone out that afternoon to stand as proxy godmother for Jane at a christening, returned to her post she found the royal apartments deserted; on asking for the queen's grace, she was told that the Lady Jane was now a prisoner detained in the Deputy Lieutenant's house.

It was there, the next day, that Jane suffered another

visit from the marquess of Winchester, now peremptorily demanding the return of all the jewels and other 'stuff' she had received from the royal stores during her nine days' reign. The Lord Treasurer went through her and Guildford's wardrobes with a cold pawnbroker's eye, confiscating jewellery, furs, hats, a velvet and sable muffler and all the money in their possession. In spite of this, a peevish inter-departmental correspondence concerning the disappearance of 'a square coffer covered with fustian of Naples', a leather box marked with Henry VIII's broad arrow and containing, among other things, thirteen pairs of worn leather gloves, and another box labelled 'the Queen's jewels' dragged on into the autumn.[2]

While Winchester was busy covering his tracks, Mr Secretary Cecil was doing the filing, methodically endorsing the office copy of a letter signed 'Jane the Quene' with the words 'Jana non Regina', and the earl of Arundel and William Paget were riding hard for Framlingham to lay the allegiance and excuses of the lords of Council at Mary Tudor's feet. Mary accepted them both. She had no choice, for, like it or not, she was going to have to rule the country with their help, and on Friday 21 July Arundel and Paget went on to Cambridge to arrest the duke of Northumberland in the queen's name. 'I beseech you, my lord of Arundel, use mercy towards me, knowing the case as it is,' said John Dudley to the man who, barely a week before, had wished he might die at his feet. 'My lord,' answered Arundel, 'ye should have sought for mercy sooner. I must do according to my commandment.'[3]

Meanwhile, in London the foreign diplomats were watching the progress of events with astonishment verging on incredulity. At the Imperial embassy they had at first been afraid that this sudden change of front might conceal some dastardly plot 'to induce my Lady to lay down her arms and then treacherously overcome her or encompass her death'; but as the days passed and they began to believe that the Lady Mary really was going to come to the throne after all, they could only ascribe her success to a miracle 'and the work of the Divine Will'.[4] Antoine de Noailles could only agree. 'The atmosphere of this country and the nature of its people are so changeable', he wrote, 'that I am compelled to make my dispatches correspondingly wavering and contradictory . . . I have witnessed the most sudden change believable in men and I believe that God alone has worked it.'[5]

More prosaically, it seems that Mary's success was due, at least in the first instance, to her unexpectedly well-organised support among the conservative and predominantly Catholic gentry of East Anglia and the Thames Valley, to her own obstinate courage and perhaps most of all to Northumberland's surprising failure to make sure of getting his hands on her before announcing Edward's death. Other factors, of course, included his own personal unpopularity, the half-hearted attitude of the other councillors and a widespread, instinctive distrust of any tampering with the rightful line of succession – especially when that tampering was so obviously for the advancement of the Dudley family. Richard Troughton, bailiff of South Walshen in the county of Lincoln, who was told of Mary's plight by his neighbour James Pratt, as they stood together by the new-scoured cattle drinking place called hedgedike, had cried aloud that it was the duke's doing 'and woe worth him that ever he was born, for he will go about to destroy all the noble blood of England'. And he drew his dagger and 'wished it at the villain's heart . . . and desired God's plague upon him, and that he might have a short life: and prayed God to save the queen's majesty, and to deliver her grace from him'.[6]

Richard Troughton may well have expressed the view of the silent majority and his prayers were certainly answered in a most satisfactory manner, for the duke's downfall could hardly have been more complete, as the Emperor's ambassadors, who witnessed his return to London on 25 July, were able to report. Armed men had been posted all along the streets to prevent the people, 'greatly excited as they were', from attacking him, and his escort had made him take off the conspicuous red cloak he wore, but he was quickly recognised and cursed as a traitor to the Crown. 'A dreadful sight it was, and a strange mutation, for those, who, a few days before, had seen the duke enter London Tower with great pomp and magnificence when the Lady Jane went there to take possession, and now saw him led like a criminal and dubbed traitor.'[7]

The entire family, the duke, the duchess and their five sons, were now safely under lock and key, but the duchess of Northumberland was released after a few days – 'sooner than expected', wrote Simon Renard – and, like the devoted wife and mother she was, immediately hurried off to meet the queen 'to move her to compassion towards her children'. But this was being too optimistic and Mary ordered her back to London, refusing to let her approach closer than five miles. The duchess of Suffolk was more fortunate. Although Suffolk had been arrested at Sheen and returned to the Tower on 28 July, the queen readily granted her cousin Frances a private audience and the duke suffered no more than a token spell in detention.

Mary made her state entry into London on 3 August, 'being brought in with her nobles very honourably and strongly'. Wearing a gown of purple velvet over a kirtle 'all thick set with goldsmith's work and great pearl . . . with a rich baldrick of gold, pearl and stones about her neck, and a rich billament of stones and great pearl on her hood,' King Henry's daughter rode in triumph through newly gravelled streets, hung with banners and streamers and lined with cheering crowds, the trumpets sounding before her.[8] Once she had been pretty: small and finely made with a delicate pink and white complexion and the Tudor family's red-gold hair. Now she was painfully thin, indelibly marked by years of unhappiness and ill-health. Her cousin's ambassadors described her as 'middling fair', but the pink and gold had long since faded, leaving a sandy-haired, tight-lipped little woman in her late thirties, with myopic grey eyes, no eyebrows and a surprisingly deep, gruff voice.

When her procession reached the Tower, the guns thundering in salute, the new queen was greeted by four kneeling figures: the old duke of Norfolk, who had been living under a suspended sentence of death ever since 1547; Stephen Gardiner, who had spent most of Edward's reign in prison on account of his unfashionable religious opinions; young Edward Courtenay, grandson of Katherine Courtenay, née Plantagenet, who had spent most of his life in prison for that reason alone; and Anne Somerset, widow of the late Protector. Mary raised the suppliants, kissed them, saying smilingly, 'these are my prisoners', and ordered their immediate release.[9] Other, more recent prisoners were not in evidence on this happy occasion. The duke of Northumberland was quartered in the Garden Tower – later popularly christened the Bloody Tower. His sons were crowded together in the Beauchamp Tower, while Jane had now been moved into the Gentleman Gaoler's house next door.

No one, it appears, had made any attempt to intercede for Jane. If her mother had taken the opportunity to speak up for her when she saw the queen at New Hall on 30 July it was not reported, and Jane herself now proceeded to write to Mary. It was a long letter, the original of which has disappeared. It survives only in an Italian translation retranslated into English, and gives Jane's own version of events from her marriage to Guildford Dudley to her early days in the Tower.

She freely admitted having done very wrong in accepting the crown and having listened to the persuasions of those who appeared at the time to be wise, 'not only to myself but also to a good part of the realm', but who had since proved the contrary. Indeed, she knew her criminal want of prudence was so serious that, 'but for the goodness and clemency of the queen', she had no hope of pardon. Jane did, though, feel there were mitigating circumstances, 'it being known that the error imputed to me has not altogether been caused by myself. Because, although my fault may be great, and I confess it to be so, nevertheless I am charged and esteemed guilty more than I have deserved. For whereas I might take upon me that of which I was not worthy, yet no one can ever say either that I sought it as my own, or that I was pleased with it.'[10]

Mary believed her. She had always had a fondness for her little cousin in spite of her heresy and her blunt outspokenness. At least you always knew where you were with Jane, and Mary, transparently honest herself, appreciated that quality in others. In fact, while her brief, incredulous glow of happiness lasted, the queen was ready to call the whole world her friend, innocently believing that the country in general hated the new ways as much as she did and that the great mass of the people were only waiting for a lead to return thankfully to the fold of the true mother church. Living for so many years in rural retreat surrounded by her Catholic household, Mary had completely failed to realise just how strongly a nationalistic form of Protestantism had taken hold in London and the south-east during the past decade, and she had seriously misinterpreted the nature of the popular welcome she had received. The people might be happy to be rid of the Dudleys and genuinely pleased to see the true line of the Tudor succession re-established, but this did not mean they were necessarily prepared to submit once more to the authority of the Bishop of Rome.

For a time Mary clung to her hopes of a peaceful reconciliation. She told the Council on 12 August that she did not wish to 'constrain other men's consciences', trusting God would put a persuasion of the truth into their hearts, and shortly afterwards a proclamation was issued in which the queen expressed her desire that the religion she herself had professed from infancy would now be quietly and charitably embraced by all her subjects; but she was not minded to compel them – not at any rate until such time 'as further order, by common consent, might be taken therein'. Meanwhile, she willed them to forbear 'those new-found devilish terms of papist or heretic'. But if Mary was prepared to be patient and listen to those who were warning her to be cautious at first in matters of religion, there were some things over which her conscience would not allow her to be cautious. She had, for example, worried a good deal about Edward's funeral, feeling it would be wrong to let her unhappy, misguided little brother go to his grave unhallowed by the rites of Holy Church. In the end she was persuaded to compromise. Archbishop Cranmer read the new English burial service over his godson in Westminster Abbey, while the queen attended a solemn requiem mass in the ancient Norman chapel in the White Tower. Mass, although still officially illegal, was now being regularly celebrated at court with the Privy Council (whose consciences were apparently as elastic as their loyalty) attending in a body, but within a month of Northumberland's fall ominous signs of a Protestant backlash had begun to manifest themselves in the streets of the capital.

The chances of establishing a lasting relationship between the Catholic queen and her independently minded subjects were not helped by Mary's obvious, understandable but unwise reliance on Simon Renard (who was to take over officially as the Emperor's resident ambassador in October) in preference to her English councillors. Renard's real business, of course, was to see off the French and rebuild the Anglo-Imperial alliance by negotiating the Spanish marriage which, in the event, would not only poison the political atmosphere but also wreck Mary's personal life beyond recovery. First, though, it was necessary to guide the inexperienced queen through the tricky opening weeks of her reign and Renard soon discovered she was quite unlike any ruler he had ever had dealings with before.

As well as urging that his 'good sister and cousin' should be advised not to be over-hasty in reforming matters of religion, the Emperor was also anxious that, for the sake of England's internal peace and quiet, Mary should, as far as possible, be magnanimous towards her enemies. 'For God's sake,' he wrote on 29 July, 'let her moderate the lust of vengeance that probably burns in her supporters who have received injuries from the other party. . . . Our cousin's great prudence will tell her that the results might be most regrettable.'[11]

But it appeared that Mary was only too ready to be magnanimous. Indeed, she would have been ready to pardon the duke of Northumberland himself if the Emperor had wished it. 'As to Jane of Suffolk, whom they tried to make queen,' wrote Renard, suppressing his exasperation with some difficulty, 'she [Mary] could not be induced to consent that she should die.' All the more so because Mary apparently believed that Jane's marriage to Guildford Dudley was invalid, 'as she was previously betrothed by a binding promise . . . to a servitor of the Bishop of Winchester'. The identity of this mysterious fiancé remains unclear, unless perhaps it was a mistake for the earl of Hertford, but in any case Mary was firmly convinced of Jane's innocence of any complicity in Northumberland's intrigues and plots. Her conscience, she declared, would not permit her to have a blameless young creature put to death.

Horrified, the ambassador pointed out as forcefully as he dared that, although Jane might be morally innocent, the fact remained that she had actually borne the title of queen – a title which could always be revived at some later date to trouble the succession to the Crown. It was also necessary to remember that, unfortunately, 'power and tyranny had sometimes more force, especially in affairs of State, than right or justice' and Renard hastily dredged up an example from Roman history when the Emperor Theodosius had felt obliged to order the execution of Maximus and Victor his son, 'notwithstanding his tender age'. But Mary was not to be moved. She did, though, promise to take 'the greatest possible care for the future' before setting the Lady Jane at liberty! Defeated, Renard could only shrug his shoulders and hope, without much conviction, that the queen would not soon have cause to regret her extraordinary clemency.[12]

There was, of course, no question of a pardon for the duke of Northumberland, and on 18 August he and his eldest son and the marquess of Northampton were tried and convicted by their peers in Westminster Hall. Next day another batch of lesser conspirators – Andrew Dudley, Sir John Gates, once Edward VI's Captain of the Guard, his brother Henry, and Thomas Palmer, Northumberland's instrument in the original attack on the Protector Somerset – were also tried and convicted, but only the duke, 'the great wheel' of the attempted coup, John Gates and Thomas Palmer actually suffered the penalty of high treason. Their execution date was fixed for Monday 21 August and all the preparations had been made when John Dudley suddenly announced that he wished to be reconciled to the Catholic faith. Whether this was from a genuine concern for his immortal soul, a desperate last-minute hope of pardon or, perhaps more likely, an attempt to save something from the wreck of his fortunes for his wife and children, the government was naturally anxious to make the most of such a valuable propaganda point, and sentence was respited for twenty-four hours to allow the duke to make his peace with God. So, at about nine o'clock on the morning of the 22nd, in a carefully staged public spectacle, Northumberland, together with the marquess of Northampton, Andrew Dudley, Henry Gates and Thomas Palmer, was escorted to the chapel of St Peter ad Vincula by Tower Green to attend mass, which, according to one rather scornful witness, was celebrated with all the elaborate business of elevation of the Host, pax giving, blessing, crossing, 'breathing', turning about, 'and all the other rites and accidents of old time appertaining'. When the time came for the prisoners to receive the sacrament, Northumberland turned to the congregation, saying: '"My masters, I let you all to understand that I do most faithfully believe this is the very right and true way, out of the which true religion you and I have been seduced this sixteen years past, by the false and erroneous preaching of the new preachers. . . . And I do believe the holy sacrament here most assuredly to be our Saviour and Redeemer Jesus Christ; and this I pray you all to testify, and pray for me." After which words he kneeled down and asked all men forgiveness, and likewise forgave all men.' The Lady Jane, added the chronicler, 'looking through the window saw the duke and the rest going to the church'.[13]

Northumberland had sent a frantic appeal to the earl of Arundel begging for his intercession:

Alas, my good lord, is my crime so heinous as no redemption but my blood can wash away the spots thereof? An old proverb there is, and that most true, that a living dog is better than a dead lion. Oh! that it would please her good grace to give me life, yea the life of a dog, if I might but live and kiss her feet and spend both life and all in her honourable services. . . . Oh! good my lord, remember how sweet life is and how bitter the contrary. Spare not your speech and pains, for God, I hope, hath not shut out all hopes of comfort from me in that gracious, princely and womanlike heart.[14]

But neither mercy nor comfort had been forthcoming and on 22 August, standing on the scaffold on Tower Hill, forty-three years almost to the day since his father had stood in the same place for the same reason, the duke repeated his solemn apostasy in the presence of a crowd of several thousand spectators and there were, it was thought, 'a large number turned with his words'. John Dudley has always had a bad press from historians and he was undoubtedly a single-mindedly ruthless and none too scrupulous political operator but, at the same time, it should in fairness be remembered that in the bitterly faction-ridden atmosphere of the time it was the strong and the ruthless who survived. Northumberland had served two generations of Tudors faithfully and had, at his trial, gone out of his way to exonerate Jane from having aspired to the crown – rather she had 'by enticement and force' been made to accept it.[15]

Not that Jane was grateful. Just a week after the duke's beheading, on Tuesday 29 August the author of *The Chronicle of Queen Jane* (generally thought to have been Rowland Lee, an official of the Royal Mint living in the Tower) dropped in to dine at the house of his friend Partridge, the Gentleman Gaoler. There he found the Lady Jane, who had chosen to eat with the family that day, sitting in the place of honour 'at the board's end', attended by her page and one of her gentlewomen. Gracious and self-possessed, Jane gave Master Partridge and his guest permission to remain covered in her presence, 'commanding Partridge and me to put on our caps', drank the visitor's health and bade him 'heartily welcome'.

Talk at the dinner table turned naturally to current affairs. 'The Queen's majesty is a merciful princess,' said Jane, who knew by this time that her life was to be spared. 'I beseech God she may long continue, and send his bountiful grace upon her.' After this, recorded the diarist, 'we fell in discourse on matters of religion'. Jane wanted to know who had preached at Paul's Cross the previous Sunday. Then she asked: 'Have they mass in London?' Yes, answered Lee cautiously, 'in some places'. 'It may be so,' said Jane. 'It is not so strange as the sudden conversion of the late duke, for who would have thought he would have so done?' 'Perchance he thereby hoped to have had his pardon,' suggested someone and thus released the floodgates of Jane's indignation. She cried out:

Pardon! Woe worth him! he hath brought me and our stock in most miserable calamity and misery by his exceeding ambition. But for the answering that he hoped for life by his turning, though other men be of that opinion, I utterly am not: for what man is there living, I pray you, although he had been innocent, that would hope for life in that case; being in the field against the queen in person as general, and after his taking so hated and evil spoken of by the commons? and at his coming into prison so wondered at [reviled] as the like was never heard by any man's time. Who was judge that he should hope for pardon, whose life was odious to all men? But what will ye more? like as his life was wicked and full of dissimulation, so was his end thereafter. I pray God, I, nor no friend of mine, die so. Should I, who am young and in my few years, forsake my faith for the love of life? Nay, God forbid! much more he should not, whose fatal course, although he had lived his just number of years, could not have long continued. But life was sweet, it appeared; so he might have lived, you will say, he did not care how. Indeed the reason is good; for he that would have lived in chains to have had his life, by like would leave no other mean [un]attempted. But God be merciful to us, for he sayeth, Whoso denieth him before men, he will not know him in his Father's kingdom.

'With this and much like talk the dinner passed away,' wrote Rowland Lee, to whom we are indebted for a splendidly revealing account of Jane Grey in full and vigorous flow. The party ended in a polite exchange of compliments, Lee thanking Lady Jane for condescending to accept him in her company and Jane thanking Partridge for bringing 'this gentleman to dinner'. 'Well, madam,' responded the Gaoler apologetically, 'we were somewhat bold, not knowing that your ladyship dined below until we found your ladyship there.' On this note of mutual courtesy the two men took their leave, Rowland Lee surely hurrying away to record his interesting experience while it was fresh in his mind.[16]

As well as vividly illustrating Lady Jane's opinion of the late duke of Northumberland and her own stern religious philosophy, Lee's account makes it clear that the conditions of her imprisonment were not too disagreeable. She was permitted a staff of four attendants – two waiting gentlewomen, Mrs Tylney and Mrs Jacob, a manservant and her old nurse, Mrs Ellen – while the sum of ninety shillings a week had been allocated out of government funds for her board and lodging, with a further allowance of twenty shillings a week for each of the servants. Partridge and his wife were treating her with respectful consideration. She was allowed to walk in the queen's garden. Nobody was bullying her and she no longer had to cope with the oppressive demands of her parents, her husband or her in-laws. She had books, peace and quiet and leisure for study, plus the queen's assurance of life and eventual liberty. Jane would not have needed to be told that, all things considered, she had escaped exceedingly lightly. But her evident pleasure at seeing a new face at the dinner table indicates that she was beginning to suffer the boredom which is the inevitable lot of every prisoner and no doubt she missed the stimulus of intellectual companionship and conversation.

Meanwhile the summer, which had been unusually hot and sultry, began to turn into autumn and life in the Gentleman Gaoler's house continued on its uneventful course. In the Tower some prisoners were released on payment of hefty fines, among them King Edward's old tutor the famous Greek scholar Sir John Cheke, and a couple of judges, Sir Roger Cholmley and Edward Montagu; while two prominent Protestant churchmen, Bishop Hugh Latimer and Archbishop Thomas Cranmer, were brought in. Some of the Dudley wives were given leave to visit their husbands, while the Dudley brothers were now being allowed to

Portrait by an unknown artist, said to be of Lady Jane Grey. (© National Portrait Gallery)

Henry Grey, 3rd Marquess of Dorset, Duke of Suffolk and father of Jane Grey – a man 'neither misliked nor much regarded' by his contemporaries. (© The British Museum)

The 2nd Marquess of Dorset began to build himself a fine new house at Bradgate Park on his Leicestershire estates, surrounded by a park of six miles in circumference, on the edge of Charnwood Forest. John Leland, who visited in the 1540s, remarked on its good and vigorous water supply and the well-wooded country round about.

(© Trevor Wickman)

The ruins of Bradgate Manor. When the Grey family abandoned Bradgate in the eighteenth century, moving their principal residence to Staffordshire, the Tudor mansion slowly fell into ruin. (© Leicester Records Office)

Henry VIII by Joos van Cleve. This is Henry in his prime when he was being described as 'the handsomest prince in Christendom'. (The Royal Collection © Her Majesty The Queen)

LA ROYNE MARIE

Mary Tudor, sister of Henry VIII, as Queen of France, probably drawn in 1515 when she was twenty years old.
*(© Ashmolean Museum, Oxford)*

Cloth of frieze matched with cloth of gold. Double portrait of Mary Tudor and Charles Brandon marking the occasion of their public wedding at Greenwich in May 1515.
*(By kind permission of the Marquess of Tavistock and the Trustees of the Bedford Estate)*

Charles Brandon, Duke of Suffolk. The king's 'dearest Brandon' was probably about fifty when this portrait was painted. (© National Portrait Gallery)

KATHARINE PARRE

Katherine Parr, the sixth wife of Henry VIII, 'who always got on pleasantly with the king and had no caprices'. (© National Portrait Gallery)

The old palace at Chelsea overlooking the Thames, on the site of the present Cheyne Walk. Built originally as a nursery for the royal children it formed part of Queen Katherine Parr's dower. (© *The Guildhall Library*)

Edward VI, the last Tudor king, who died in 1553 at the age of fifteen. *(The Royal Collection © Her Majesty The Queen)*

Queen Mary Tudor who once described herself as 'the most unhappy lady in Christendom'. *(Mary Evans Picture Library)*

The Princess Elizabeth painted by an unknown artist round about the time of her father's death. *(The Royal Collection © Her Majesty The Queen)*

Katherine Parr's tomb at Sudeley Castle in Gloucestershire.
*(Photograph © Lara E. Eakins)*

Thomas Seymour, the dashing Lord Admiral – 'fierce in courage, courtly in fashion; in personage stately, in voice magnificent, but somewhat empty of matter'. *(Mary Evans Picture Library)*

Jane Grey and Roger Ascham: artist's impression of the famous occasion when Ascham found Jane reading Plato 'with as much delight as some gentleman would read a merry tale in Boccaccio'. (© *National Portrait Gallery*)

John Dudley, Viscount Lisle, earl of Warwick, duke of Northumberland, who married his son Guildford to Lady Jane Grey and used her as his pawn in his bid for power. (*Bridgeman Art Library/Ken Welsh*)

Carving on the wall of the Beauchamp Tower, said to be the work of John, the eldest surviving Dudley brother and showing the family badge of the bear and ragged staff. *(Crown Copyright: Historic Royal Palace)*

The Beauchamp Tower in the Tower of London, where several of the Dudley brothers were imprisoned after their father's failed *coup d'état*. *(© The Guildhall Library)*

Edward's 'Device for the Succession', in which he disinherited his half-sisters Mary and Elizabeth and bequeathed the crown to 'the Lady Jane and her heirs masles'. (© The Masters of the Bench of the Inner Temple)

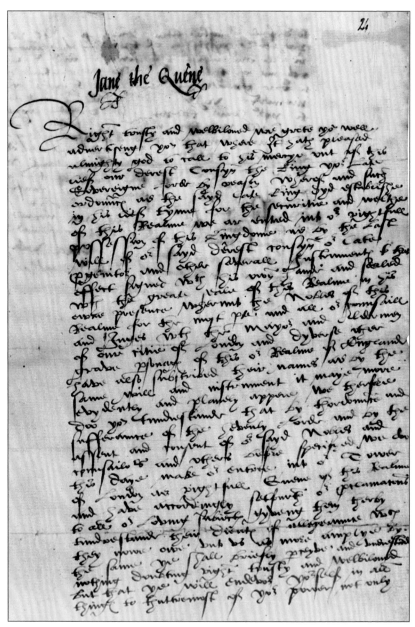

One of the Letters Patent issued over the sign manual of Queen Jane and which was later endorsed 'Jana non Regina' by Mr Secretary William Cecil.
*(© The British Library)*

The songe of Saynt Ambrose. Praise the

God we knowlege the to be the Lord

All the earthe doughe worshyp the, whiche arte the father everlasting

To the cryeth all angells, the heavens, and all the powers therein

To the thus cryeth Cherubin

Cherubin and Seraphyn contynually

of arte thou of arte
thou of arte thou

thine arte the lord god of
hostes.

heaven and earthe are full

Let is the glorie of thi magestie

The glorious company of ti
apostells praise the

The godly felowshyppe of the
prophetes worshyp the

The fayre felowshyppe of mar
ters praise the

The holy congregacion of

Forasmuche as you have desired so symple
a woman to wyshe i so worthy i lord as
a fervent desyre you had last to...
you to call uppon god to enflame...
his lawes to quicken you in his waye

Jane Grey's prayer book, which she carried with her to the scaffold and in which she had written a farewell message to the Lieutenant of the Tower – 'Yours, as the Lord knoweth as a friend, Jane Duddeley.' (© *The British Library*)

The Execution of Lady Jane Grey: an imaginative depiction of a scene which actually took place in daylight on Tower Green.
(© *Bridgeman Art Library*)

The Tower of London, showing the Yeoman Gaoler's house and the Green, where Jane Grey was beheaded. *(Crown Copyright: Historic Royal Palaces)*

Lady Katherine Grey, Jane Grey's younger sister, with Edward, her elder son by Edward Seymour, earl of Hertford, born in the Tower of London in September 1561. *(The Collection of the Duke of Northumberland)*

Wedding portrait of Jane Grey's mother, Frances, dowager duchess of Suffolk, with her second husband Adrian Stokes, said to have been her Master of the Horse and sixteen years her junior, painted by Hans Eworth. (© Royal Academy of Arts)

exercise on the leads – that is, on the roof of their prison. At the end of September there was a renewed flurry of activity in the royal apartments as the court came briefly back into residence preparatory to the queen's coronation and the traditional eve-of-coronation Recognition Procession through the city to Westminster. None of this had anything to do with Jane. Her sixteenth birthday came and went and she remained, apparently forgotten, in her quarters overlooking Tower Green.

The first parliament of the new reign met on 5 October and one of its first acts was to repeal the 1534 Act of Succession and declare the marriage of the queen's parents to have been good and lawful after all. It also repealed all the religious legislation passed in her brother's time, thus in effect returning the English church to the state in which Henry VIII had left it, which well suited all those members of both Houses who had done so nicely out of the general share-out of church property in the 1540s. By and large it also satisfied the silent majority who had disliked the desecration of their parish churches and the violence of the more militant reformers. It was less acceptable to the militants themselves and already there had been hostile demonstrations at the weekly sermons at Paul's Cross.

James Haddon, that earnest professor of the gospel, was deeply saddened by the new turn of events. 'Alas! what a severe loss have we sustained!' he wrote to Henry Bullinger on 30 November. 'Alas! how true religion is banished! Alas! how justly is the wrath of God stirred up against us! I dare not write more; you must understand the rest. . . . Pour forth your prayers, I entreat you, for me and those like me. . . . What will be the result, God knows, and whether this may not be the last letter that I shall be able to write to you. . . .'[17]

In fact, Haddon was soon to join the exodus of committed Protestants who took themselves and their consciences to the more congenial climates of Strasburg, Zurich and

Geneva during what was to become known as the Marian Reaction. On the other hand Dr Harding, also once domestic chaplain to the Suffolk family, had 'fallen from the truth of God's most Holy Word' and followed his more prudent brethren back into the shelter of the Roman fold, thus incurring the freely expressed censure of his former pupil. Jane wrote:

> I cannot but marvel at thee and lament thy case, who seemed sometime to be the lively member of Christ, but now the deformed imp of the devil; sometime the beautiful temple of God, but now the stinking and filthy kennel of Satan; sometime the unspotted spouse of Christ, but now the unshamefaced paramour of AntiChrist; sometime my faithful brother, but now a stranger and apostate; sometime a stout Christian soldier, but now a cowardly runaway.[18]

Nineteenth-century biographers of Jane Grey had some difficulty with this sustained piece of invective, which does not exactly fit in with the received image of their heroine; and they made strenuous efforts to dissociate her from the 'vulgar polemic' of this 'coarsely violent epistle', refusing to believe that such unbecoming language could have issued from the mind or pen of an amiable young female. Jane's own contemporaries took a more robust view and welcomed the Harding letter – which was later printed both as a popular pamphlet and in John Foxe's best-selling *Book of Martyrs* – as proceeding from the zealous heart of a justly aggrieved Christian lady. The Elizabethans saw nothing unbecoming in such epithets as 'sink of sin', 'child of perdition' or even 'white-livered milksop' being applied to someone who had let the side down as badly as Harding had done.

> 'Wherefore hast thou instructed others to be strong in Christ . . .' demanded the aggrieved Christian lady 'when

thou thyself dost rather choose to live miserably (with shame) in this world, than to die gloriously and reign in honour with Christ to the end of all eternity? . . . Oh wretched and unhappy man what art thou but dust and ashes, and wilt thou resist thy maker, that formed and fashioned thee; wilt thou now forsake him that called thee . . . to be an ambassador and messenger of his eternal word? . . . How canst thou, having knowledge, or how darest thou neglect the law of the Lord and follow the vain tradition of men, and whereas thou hast been a public professor of his name, become now a defacer of his glory? Wilt thou refuse the true God, and worship the invention of man, the golden calf, the whore of Babylon, the Romish religion, the abominable idol, the most wicked mass? Wilt thou torment again, rend and tear the most precious body of our Saviour Christ with thy bodily and fleshly teeth, without the breaking whereof upon the cross, our sins and transgressions could else no way be redeemed? . . . Can neither the punishment of the Israelites . . . nor the terrible threatenings of the prophets, nor the curses of God's own mouth, fear thee to honour any other god than him?[19]

Jane went on to batter her target with a barrage of texts from the Old and New Testaments, before exhorting him to repentance:

Disdain not to come again with the lost son, seeing you have so wandered with him: be not ashamed to turn again with him from the swill of strangers . . . acknowledging that you have sinned against heaven and earth. . . . Be not abashed to come again with Mary and to weep bitterly with Peter, not only with shedding of tears out of your bodily eyes, but also pouring out the streams of your heart, to wash away, out of the sight of God, the filth and mire of your offensive fall. Be not abashed to say with the publican, 'Lord be merciful unto me a sinner'. . . . Last of all, let the lively remembrance of the last day be always before your eyes, remembering the terror that such shall be in at that time, with the runagates and fugitives from Christ . . . and contrariwise, the inestimable joys prepared for them that, fearing no peril, nor dreading death, have manfully fought and victoriously triumphed over all power of darkness, over hell, death and damnation through their most redoubted captain, Christ, who now stretcheth out his arms to receive you.[20]

The effect of this onslaught on Dr Harding does not appear to have been recorded but his regrettable defection was certainly not an isolated case. The great majority of parish priests seem to have reverted uncomplainingly, or with relief, to the familiar rituals of King Henry's day, taking their flocks with them. In the more remote and rural parts of the country the drastic changes of the past five years had, after all, scarcely had time to take root, but in London it was different. The foreign congregations were already leaving and some of the more outspoken preachers had been arrested. The Revd Thomas Mountain, of St Michael's Paternoster, got into serious trouble with the newly restored bishop of Winchester for having celebrated communion according to the 1552 Prayer Book on the Sunday following the coronation, and on 6 December, the day parliament rose, a dead dog, tonsured like a priest and a rope round its neck 'with a scandalous writing attached to it, signifying that the priests and bishops should be hanged', was thrown into Mary's presence chamber. 'The Queen', wrote Simon Renard, 'was displeased at this, and told Parliament that such acts might move her to a kind of justice further removed from clemency than she could wish.'[21]

Renard, who tended to see rebellious heretics behind every bush, was already worried that Mary's insistence on following a policy of clemency and of substituting fines for executions was being interpreted as weakness. 'Her authority has suffered from the pecuniary compositions for offences, and people have come to judge her actions so freely that they go so far as to laugh at them.' It was for this reason, so he heard, that the queen had now decided to take a different course, 'and to order the four sons of the duke of Northumberland, and Jane of Suffolk, to be tried and sentenced to receive capital punishment for the crimes they have committed'.[22] This dispatch was dated 19 September, but it was mid-November before Jane finally stood trial, her co-defendants being her husband, two of his brothers, Ambrose and Henry, and Archbishop Thomas Cranmer.

The little procession, headed by the Archbishop, was escorted through the streets to the Guildhall by the Lieutenant of the Tower and a force of four hundred halberdiers, and preceded by the chief Gentleman Warder carrying the axe. Lady Jane was dressed entirely in black – black cloth gown, a cape lined and trimmed with velvet, a French hood, also black with a velvet billament or border, a prayer book bound in black velvet hanging from her girdle and another book of devotions held open in her hands – and walked behind her husband, her two women servants attending her. The proceedings, held before an impressive array of peers and judges, were brief and formal. The defendants pleaded guilty to the charges of high treason and sentence was duly pronounced by Richard Morgan, newly appointed Chief Justice of the Common Pleas: hanging, drawing and quartering for Cranmer and the Dudley brothers; burning or beheading at the queen's pleasure for Jane. Then came the return journey to the Tower, the edge of the headsman's axe now turned towards the prisoners.[23] But it was still by no means certain when, or even whether, the sentence would be carried out. Already another fate was being reserved for Thomas Cranmer, while the general opinion remained that Lady Jane and the young Dudleys would be spared. 'It is believed that Jane will not die,' wrote Simon Renard on the day after the trial; and again, three days later: 'As for Jane, I am told her life is safe.'[24]

The social position of the Grey family in the late autumn of 1553 must surely have been uniquely unusual. While her eldest daughter and son-in-law remained in the Tower, convicted traitors under sentence of death, albeit a suspended sentence, the duchess of Suffolk was to be found preening herself at court, apparently in high favour. On at least one occasion that winter the queen had chosen to give her cousin Frances precedence over her sister Elizabeth, with whom she was on increasingly bad terms. In his eagerness to cut his connections with the Greys, the earl of Pembroke had repudiated his son's marriage with the Lady Katherine and packed her off back to her parents; and Katherine – who was growing into a very pretty girl, the only one of the sisters to have inherited some of their Tudor grandmother's famous beauty – was now at court with her mother, she and plain little Mary Grey having been admitted to the privileged ranks of the queen's maids of honour. Even the duke of Suffolk, reported Renard on 17 November, had 'made his confession as to religion' and as a result had been let off (after paying a fine of £20,000) and reinstated in polite society by means of a general pardon.[25] Although Renard continued to regard all the Greys with the deepest suspicion – almost as much as he did the sly and heretical Princess Elizabeth – it is hardly surprising that in the circumstances Lady Jane's trial should have been regarded as little more than a formality and her release expected to be no more than a matter of time.

But even before Jane stood in the Guildhall to hear verdict and sentence pronounced upon her, the chain of events that would lead to her death had begun its inexorable progression.

'In the beginning of November was the first notice among the people touching the marriage of the Queen to the King of Spain,' noted *The Chronicle of Queen Jane*, and as it became generally known that Mary intended to marry her cousin Philip, son and heir of the Emperor Charles V, rumbles of disapproval, ominous as distant thunder, were immediately audible. Some people, indeed, were moved to wonder if the late unlamented duke of Northumberland was going to be proved right after all, for Philip was not merely a foreigner and a Roman Catholic – he represented the most formidable Catholic power bloc in Europe.

No responsible person, of course, questioned that the queen should marry. The idea of a single woman attempting to govern a people so notoriously unruly as the English was not to be thought of. Obviously she must have a husband to guide, comfort and protect her and undertake, as Renard delicately put it, those duties which were 'not within woman's province', but in the opinion of the great majority of her subjects her wisest choice of consort would have been Edward Courtenay, the last sprig of the white Plantagenet rose. Courtenay, now in his mid-twenties, had high birth, good looks, good manners and plenty of personal charm to recommend him: '*Le plus beau et plus agreable gentilhomme d'Angleterre*', commented Antoine de Noailles approvingly.

Mary had released Courtenay from the Tower and created him earl of Devonshire – his only crime, after all, lay in being the great-grandson of Edward IV, and his parents had been among Queen Catherine of Aragon's most devoted friends – but although she was quite prepared to be kind to him, she made it clear that she had no intention of marrying him – or any other Englishman for that matter. Tragically, nothing in her experience had ever given her cause to love or trust her own countrymen. Ever since her unhappy teens she had been forced to rely on her mother's kin for advice and support, and now the fact that Philip of

Spain, a widower at twenty-six, happened to be the most brilliant match in Europe undoubtedly weighed far less with her than the fact that he was also the grandson of her mother's sister.

Mary had not reached her decision lightly. Renard had first broached the subject of marriage to her in a general way as early as the end of July and it had taken him three months of patient tactful persuasion, three months of slipping in and out of back doors and up the privy stairs for quiet late evening talks to reassure the nervous queen and overcome her maidenly shrinking, her self-doubts and fears that Philip was too young for her – or she too old for him – and that in her ignorance of 'that which was called love' she would not be able to satisfy him; for, as she shyly confessed, she had never 'harboured thoughts of voluptuousness, and had never considered marriage until God had been pleased to raise her to the throne . . .'. If the prince 'were disposed to be amorous', she said on another occasion, 'such was not her desire', for she was of the age the Emperor knew of 'and had never harboured thoughts of love'.[26]

Although one of the reasons publicly advanced in favour of the queen's marriage was to secure an heir to safeguard the succession, not many people seriously believed that Mary, at her age and with her medical history, would ever bear a child. Mary herself was not so sure. God had already worked one miracle for her. Might he not be planning to work another, to give her a son – a future Catholic king of England? For with Philip at her side and all the might of the Holy Roman Empire behind her, surely nothing could prevent her from carrying out God's manifest purpose of leading her country back into the arms of the true Church? When, therefore, at the end of October 1553, after weeks of heart-searching and prayer, the queen finally pledged her word to Renard in the presence of the Holy Sacrament that she would marry Philip and love him perfectly, it was done with desperate sincerity and in the conviction that her answer had been divinely inspired. The fact that, despite her protestations, after so many years of barren loneliness and rejection she also yearned on a very human level to love and be loved could not of course be admitted, perhaps least of all to herself.

Knowledge of the queen's intentions was already causing consternation, both in parliament and among her councillors. Stephen Gardiner, now Lord Chancellor, and her old friends Edward Waldegrave and Francis Englefield came to see her to plead Courtenay's cause. Gardiner based his argument on the assertion that as the country 'never would abide a foreigner, Courtenay was the only possible match for her'. Englefield went so far as to point out that Philip had a kingdom of his own and would not wish to leave it to come to England, while Waldegrave said bluntly that a Spanish marriage would be bound to mean war with France.[27]

These were cogent, logical arguments but they had little effect on Mary, and she was equally unimpressed by a parliamentary deputation, led by the Speaker of the Commons, which waited on her in November to beg her to marry one of her own subjects. Her marriage was entirely her own affair, she told them sharply. Parliament, however well meaning, 'was not accustomed to use such language to the kings of England, nor was it suitable or respectful that it should do so. . . . Moreover', she went on in a burst of petulance, 'to force her to take a husband who would not be to her liking would be to cause her death, for if she were married against her will she would not live three months, and would have no children, wherefore the Speaker would be defeating his own ends.'[28]

The deputation was silenced but the Commons continued to grumble among themselves. When someone mentioned that the nation could protect itself by the 'bonds and covenants which this prince should enter into with the queen', someone else stood up and asked a 'smart question'.

What would happen if the bands should be broken between the husband and wife, both of them being princes in their own country? 'Who shall be their judges? and what shall be the advantage?' To which the answer came: 'None, but discord, dissension, war, bloodshed, and either extreme enmity, or else that one part must at length break or yield.'[29]

The only Englishman who might have been able to get Mary to see the sort of trouble she was storing up for herself was Stephen Gardiner but, again unhappily, there was little trust or ease of communication between them. Mary could not forget the part that Gardiner as bishop of Winchester had once played in helping her father to divorce her mother and Gardiner, faced with a stubborn, emotional woman who had already given her confidence elsewhere, seems to have lacked both nerve and stomach for doing battle. He could argue forcefully enough with Renard but to Mary could only object rather lamely that the people would not put up with a foreigner, who would make promises that he would not keep once the marriage had been concluded. The queen retorted that her mind was made up, and if her Chancellor preferred the will of the people to her wishes, then he was not keeping *his* promises. Stephen Gardiner, with his long and bitter experience of Tudor temperament, retreated, saying the matter was too dangerous to meddle with. He was, in any case, handicapped by his known partiality for Courtenay, to whom he had become much attached while they were in the Tower together. As Mary rather unkindly remarked, was it reasonable to expect her to marry someone just because the bishop had made friends with him in prison, and, so Renard heard, she went on to speak of 'the designs of the French, Courtenay's small power and authority, and the poverty of the kingdom, until the Chancellor told her that it would not be right to try to force her in one direction or another, and that he would obey the man she had chosen'.[30]

Across the Channel the French were taking a deeply gloomy view of the situation. Faced with the prospect of seeing his good sister the queen of England married to his greatest enemy, King Henri II was not convinced by Mary's assurances that she meant to continue to live in peace and amity with her neighbours no matter whom she married. As he remarked to her ambassador Nicholas Wotton in December: 'It is to be considered that a husband may do much with his wife; and it shall be very hard for any wife to refuse her husband anything that he shall earnestly require of her.' Wotton had been about in the world, the king went on, and knew how subtle and crafty the Spaniards were.[31] Indeed, the danger that England would be dragged into war with France was one of the most serious and, as it turned out, well-founded objections to the Spanish match.

In drawing up his son's marriage treaty, Charles V was leaning over backwards in his efforts to take account of the delicate susceptibilities of the English and Philip himself was being instructed to choose his retinue with the greatest care, bearing in mind that they would be going to a country where strangers were not liked. 'It is impossible', wrote the Emperor, 'to exaggerate the importance, both for present and future purposes, of gaining popularity and goodwill.' Philip, too, must remember from the outset to 'converse and be friendly with the English, behaving to them in a cordial manner'.[32] Unfortunately, despite these good intentions, the English were currently in the grip of one of their periodic attacks of xenophobia, and many otherwise quite level-headed people were allowing themselves to be carried away by the scaremongering of such interested parties as the French ambassador and the radical Protestants, who were busy spreading rumours that a horde of Spaniards, all armed to the teeth, was poised to invade their shores, and that England was about to become a province of the Empire with the Pope's authority reimposed by force. Nor were professors of the Gospel reassured by the fact that as from 20 December the Latin mass, such as was 'most commonly used in the realm of England in the last year of the reign of our late sovereign lord King Henry VIII', would again become the only legal form of divine service and married priests would no longer be allowed to minister to their parishioners.

As the year drew to a close public alarm and suspicion were reaching the point where Antoine de Noailles felt the time had come to indicate how the situation could most profitably be exploited. Mary might have refused Courtenay, but there was always Elizabeth, 'and from what I hear', he wrote to the French king on 14 December, 'it only requires that my Lord Courtenay should marry her, and that they should go together to the counties of Devonshire and Cornwall. Here it can easily be believed that they would find many adherents, and they could then make a strong claim to the crown, and the Emperor and the Prince of Spain would find it difficult to suppress this rising.'

Certainly Elizabeth and Courtenay would have made a powerful combination. Indeed, the romantic appeal of this handsome, well-matched young couple, both of the English blood royal, ought to have been irresistible – but for one serious snag. 'The misfortune', admitted de Noailles, 'is that the said Courtenay is of such a fearful and timid disposition that he dare not make the venture.'[33] It was exasperating when so many influential people would have been willing to help, but there was no denying the fact that, for all his patrician breeding and winning ways, Courtenay had turned out to be a poor creature, with a vicious streak beneath the charm. He was plainly untrustworthy and would doubtless go to pieces in a crisis. However, de Noailles, who had to work with the material available, continued to hope that, carefully handled, he would make a useful tool. As for Elizabeth, the ambassador seems to have taken her cooperation for granted. Whether he had any grounds, other than his own wishful thinking, for making this assumption it is impossible to say; but if the princess ever did seriously contemplate raising a rebellion against her sister, the chicken-hearted Courtenay was surely the last person with whom she would willingly have joined forces.

Nevertheless, ambitious plans for armed resistance against the proud Spaniard and 'the coming in of him or his favourers' were now being laid. They were still maturing on 2 January when the Imperial envoys, led by Count Egmont, arrived 'for the knitting up of the marriage of the queen to the King of Spain'. Egmont and his colleagues landed at the Tower wharf to be greeted by 'a great peal of guns' from the Tower batteries, while on Tower Hill a reception committee headed by Edward Courtenay was waiting to conduct them ceremoniously through the city to Westminster, but 'the people, nothing rejoicing, held down their heads sorrowfully'. On the previous day the embassy servants had been pelted with snowballs, but at least nothing was actually thrown at the distinguished visitors.[34]

The treaty was signed on 12 January 1554 and three days later Stephen Gardiner addressed the assembled court in the presence chamber at Westminster, informing them officially of the queen's forthcoming marriage and promising that 'the queen should rule in all things as she doth now; and that there should be of the council no Spaniard, neither should [any Spaniard] have the custody of any forts or castles; neither bear rule or office in the queen's house or elsewhere in all England'.[35] Philip was to observe all the laws and customs of the country, and if Mary died first he would have no claim on the realm.

This should have been enough to satisfy the most exacting Englishman, but unfortunately the rising tide of panic and prejudice sweeping the country could no longer be stemmed by reason. The mindless rallying cry – 'We will have no foreigner for our king' – had temporarily driven out common sense, and within a week word reached London that Sir Peter Carew was up in Devonshire 'resisting of the King of Spain's coming'. Almost simultaneously news came in that Sir Thomas Wyatt, son of the poet, was up in Kent 'for the said quarrel, in resisting the said King of Spain'; that Sir James Crofts had departed for Wales 'as it is thought to raise his power there'; and that the duke of Suffolk and his brothers had mysteriously vanished from Sheen.

The fourfold rising had originally been timed for March – to coincide with better weather and the expected date of Philip's arrival – but that 'young fool of a Lord Courtenay', always the weak link, had lost what little nerve he possessed and blabbed to Gardiner; either that, or the Lord Chancellor, becoming suspicious, had wormed a confession out of his protégé. At any rate, he told all he knew about 'the enterprise of Peter Carew and his companions'.[36] The other conspirators, not knowing to what extent their plans had been betrayed, but too deeply committed to draw back, were thus scrambled into premature action.

The movement in the West Country had always depended heavily for success on Courtenay's presence, on the prestige of his name and his strong family connections with the area. Without him it died at birth and Peter Carew was obliged to leave hurriedly for France, while James Crofts never even got as far as Wales. But in Kent things were different. By 26 January Thomas Wyatt and his friends had taken possession of Rochester and the crews of the royal ships lying in the Medway had gone over to him with their guns and ammunition.

A hastily mustered force, consisting of men of the queen's guard and the city's trained bands under the command of that ancient warhorse the duke of Norfolk, was dispatched to counter the threat, but the Londoners and a good proportion of the guard promptly defected to the rebels amid rousing cries of 'We are all Englishmen!' In the words of one Alexander Brett, they preferred to spend their blood in the quarrel of 'this worthy captain Master Wyatt' and prevent at all costs the approach of the proud Spaniards who, as every right-thinking Englishman knew, would treat them like slaves, despoil them of their goods and lands, ravish their wives before their faces and deflower their daughters in their presence.[37]

Thus encouraged, Wyatt pressed on towards the capital and on 30 January he was camped around Blackheath and Greenwich, putting London into an uproar of alarm and confusion, and for a couple of tense days the loyalty of the citizens hung in the balance. It was Mary herself who really saved the situation. Reacting like a true Tudor, she ignored advice to seek her own safety and marched into the city to make a fighting speech in the crowded Guildhall that not even Elizabeth could have bettered. 'I am come' she said, 'in mine own person, to tell you what you already see and know, how traitorously and rebelliously a number of Kentish men have assembled against us and you. . . .' All this pother about her marriage, she declared scornfully, was no more than a 'Spanish cloak' to cover an attack on her religion and she went on:

Now, loving subjects, what I am ye right well know – I am your Queen, to whom at my coronation, when I was wedded to the realm and the laws of the same, you pronounced your allegiance and obedience. And that I am the right and true inheritor of the crown, I take all Christendom to witness. My father possessed the same regal estate, and to him ye always showed yourselves most faithful and loving subjects; and, therefore, I doubt not that ye will so show yourselves likewise to me. . . . Good subjects, pluck up your hearts, and like true men stand fast against these rebels, both our enemies and yours; and fear them not, for I assure you, I fear them nothing at all.[38]

Her audience rose to her, and when Wyatt reached Southwark on 3 February he found the bridge closed and defended against him.

It was a long time since London had last had an army

at its gates and 'much noise and tumult was everywhere' as shops were shuttered, market stalls hastily dismantled and weapons unearthed from store. Children stared wide-eyed at the Lord Mayor and his aldermen riding about the streets in unaccustomed battle array, 'aged men were astonished' and women wept for fear.[39] The queen had refused to allow the Tower guns to be turned on the rebels in case the innocent inhabitants of Southwark were harmed, and after three days' uneasy stalemate Wyatt withdrew his men from the bridge foot, marching them upriver to Kingston, where they crossed to the northern bank and turned eastward again. But the steam had gone out of them now. They were tired and hungry and too much time had been wasted. Yet still they came trudging on through the western suburbs, reaching Knightsbridge on the morning of Ash Wednesday, 7 February. There followed some rather indecisive skirmishing with the royal forces, commanded by the earl of Pembroke, round St James and Charing Cross, and there was some panic at Whitehall when, in the general turmoil, a cry of treason was raised within the palace as a rumour spread that Pembroke had gone over to the enemy. 'There', remarked one observer, 'should ye have seen running and crying of ladies and gentlewomen, shutting of doors, and such a shrieking and noise as it was wonderful to hear.' But although her very presence chamber was full of armed men and the sporadic gunfire from Charing Cross was clearly audible, the queen stood fast, sending word that she would tarry to see the uttermost. She asked for the earl of Pembroke and was told he was in the field. 'Well then,' answered Mary, 'fall to prayer, and I warrant you we shall hear better news anon; for my lord will not deceive me I know well.'

On this occasion, at least, her confidence was not misplaced. Wyatt and some of his followers got through Temple Bar and on down Fleet Street, but found Ludgate barred and strongly held by Lord William Howard, the Lord Admiral. It was the end for Wyatt. He himself had 'kept touch', as he said, but when it came to the point his friends in the city had failed him. He sat for a while in the rain on a bench outside the Belle Sauvage inn and then, realising it was hopeless, turned back towards Charing Cross. Fighting flared again briefly as Pembroke's men came up and the men round Wyatt prepared to sell their lives dearly, but the bloodshed was stopped by Norroy herald who approached Wyatt and begged him to give himself up, rather than 'be the death of all these your soldiers', and adding: 'Perchance ye may find the queen merciful.' Wyatt, soaked, exhausted and confused, hesitated for a moment and then yielded.[40]

The rebellion was over and the grim business of rounding up the prisoners began. But the queen's troubles were only just beginning, for either she must bow to the will of the people, so violently expressed, and abandon her marriage plans, or she must stand firm. Mary did not hesitate. Deeply hurt, angry and bewildered, she knew she must stand firm and that meant she could no longer afford the luxury of showing mercy.

# SIX

## THE END OF THE LADY JANE

If my faults deserve punishment, my youth at least and my imprudence were worthy of excuse. God and posterity will show me favour.

Jane Grey

Jane of Suffolk and her husband were to lose their heads, might indeed have already done so, wrote Simon Renard to the Emperor on the day after that momentous Ash Wednesday.[1] It was, of course, inevitable that Jane Grey would be the first victim of the government's new hard-line policy. Innocent she might have been of any complicity in the duke of Northumberland's coup, and innocent she undoubtedly was of complicity in Wyatt's rebellion – but this did not alter the fact that her continued existence had now come to represent an unacceptable danger to the state. Her own father's recent behaviour alone made that abundantly clear.

Henry Grey, duke of Suffolk, who owed his life and liberty entirely to Mary's generosity, had repaid her by attempting to raise the midland shires against her marriage and had been deeply involved with Wyatt. Summoned to court on 26 January, he told the messenger that he was on the point of hastening to the queen's side. 'Marry', quoth he, 'I was coming to her grace. Ye may see I am booted and spurred ready to ride; and I will but break my fast and go.'[2] Instead he rode northwards and was next heard of at

Stony Stratford. He subsequently turned up in the towns of Leicester and Melton Mowbray, issuing proclamations against the Spanish marriage and 'to avoid strangers out of the realm', but he gathered little or no support. 'I trust your grace meaneth no hurt to the queen's majesty,' said the mayor of Leicester anxiously. No, no, answered Suffolk, laying his hand on his sword. 'He that would [do] her any hurt, I would this sword were through his heart, for she is the mercifullest prince, as I have truly found her . . . in whose defence I am and will be ready to die at her foot.'[3] All the same, Coventry barred its gates to him and by this time the earl of Huntingdon was in hot pursuit.

Increasingly isolated, and 'perceiving himself destitute of all such aid as he looked for among his friends in the two shires of Leicester and Warwick', the duke fled to his nearby manor of Astley, where he and his brother John 'bestowed themselves in secret places' within the park.[4] The story goes that they were betrayed by a keeper named Underwood, and that the duke was found concealed in the trunk of a hollow tree and Lord John buried under a pile of hay. Some accounts add the picturesque detail that the duke's hiding place was sniffed out by a dog, whose barking led the hunters to their quarry.[5]

The assertion that Suffolk had re-proclaimed his daughter during this unprofitable excursion round the shires appears to be false – certainly it is explicitly denied by the *Chronicles* of Holinshed and Stowe. But either way it hardly matters. What did matter was that Jane had been nominated as heir by the late King Edward, who was now equipped with a fully formed Protestant halo, and that she had once been publicly proclaimed queen. What was more likely, in the present highly volatile political situation, than that she might again be used as the figurehead of some Protestant plot? Few people urged this view more strongly than men like the earls of Arundel, Pembroke and Winchester, so recently prominent Protestant plotters themselves, and who – with the prospect of the imminent arrival of a strong-minded Spanish consort before them – were more than ever anxious to see any awkward reminders of their past indiscretions permanently obliterated. 'They that were sworn chief of the council with the Lady Jane, and caused the Queen [Mary] to be proclaimed a bastard through all England,' wrote a contemporary (he was Bishop Ponet, Gardiner's successor in the see of Winchester), '. . . afterwards became counsellors, I will not say procurers, of the innocent Lady Jane's death: and at this present are in the highest authority in the Queen's house.'[6] This seems to indicate that even at this eleventh hour Mary would have saved Jane if she could, but neither Mary, for all her obstinate, conscientious courage, nor Jane, with her formidable intellectual capacity and passionate intensity of conviction, was a match for the desperate, ruthless men who surrounded them. Both in their different ways were the helpless prisoners of their circumstances.

Guildford Dudley was to die with his wife, and their execution date was originally fixed for Friday 9 February. But although the queen had been unable to save her cousin's life, she was determined to make a last-minute effort to save her soul, and Dr Feckenham, the new Dean of St Paul's, was sent over to the Tower with a few days' grace to see what he could do with this especially obdurate heretic. In his late thirties, comfortably stout and pink-faced, John Feckenham had a reputation for persuasiveness. A kind-hearted man, able and sensible, he was also unusually liberal for a cleric in that embattled age. Jane received him politely, telling him that he was welcome, if his coming was to give Christian exhortation, and prepared to engage in the stimulating cut and thrust of theological debate for what would surely be the last time. But when Feckenham began by expressing sympathy for her 'heavy case', she cut him short. 'As for my heavy case, I thank God, I do so little lament it that rather I account the same for a more manifest declaration of

God's favour toward me, than ever he showed me at any time before.' Therefore, there was no need for anyone to lament or be grieved over her present predicament, it 'being a thing so profitable for my soul's health'.

She defended the Protestant doctrine of justification by faith alone, parrying Feckenham's 'St Paul saith, "If I have all faith without love, it is nothing",' with a sharp retort: 'True it is; for how can I love him whom I trust not, or how can I trust him whom I love not? Faith and love go both together, and yet love is comprehended in faith.' Of course it was right for a Christian to do good works 'in token that he followeth his master Christ'. But 'when we have done all, yet we be unprofitable servants, and faith only in Christ's blood saveth us'.

The discussion then touched on the correct scriptural number of sacraments. Jane would only allow two – the sacrament of baptism, by which 'I am washed with water . . . and that washing is a token to me that I am the child of God'; and the sacrament of the Lord's supper, 'a sure seal and testimony that I am, by the blood of Christ, which he shed for me on the cross, made partaker of the everlasting kingdom'.

'Why? What do you receive in that sacrament?' demanded Feckenham. 'Do you not receive the very body and blood of Christ?' This, of course, was always the crux of any argument between the two creeds, and Jane's response came prompt and confident. 'No, surely I do not so believe. I think that at the supper I neither receive flesh nor blood, but bread and wine; which bread when it is broken, and the wine when it is drunken, put me in remembrance how for my sins the body of Christ was broken, and his blood shed on the cross.'

'Why', protested Feckenham, 'doth not Christ speak these words, "Take, eat, this is my body"? Require you any plainer words? Doth he not say it is his body?' 'And so he saith, "I am the vine, I am the door",' retorted Jane; 'but he is never the more for that the door or the vine. Doth not St Paul say, "He calleth things that are not, as though they were"?' Surely anyone should be able to recognise figurative speech for what it was. And now she went over to the attack: 'I pray you to answer me to this one question. Where was Christ when he said, "Take, eat, this is my body"? Was he not at the table when he said so? He was at that time alive, and suffered not till the next day. What took he but bread? What brake he but bread? And what gave he but bread?'

When Feckenham objected that she was grounding her faith 'upon such authors as say and unsay both in a breath; and not upon the church' the reply came again with the authentic ring of total, terrifying conviction: 'I ground my faith on God's word and not upon the church . . . the faith of the church must be tried by God's word; and not God's word by the church, neither yet my faith.'

Feckenham was reluctant to admit defeat in the battle to secure this so desirable convert and continued the argument with 'many strong and logical persuasions'; but faith, wrote Jane, had armed her resolution against words, and to forsake that faith for love of life, as her old dread Northumberland had done, would still have been the ultimate shame for this eager, vital sixteen-year-old.

The account of the confrontation with Feckenham, which has come down to us in the robustly Protestant pages of John Foxe, naturally gives Jane the last word and the victory; but Jane herself, who accepted Feckenham's offer to accompany her to the scaffold, parted from him with some regret, since they plainly could not look forward to resuming their discussion in the hereafter. Unless, of course, he were to repent and turn to God. She would, she told him, 'pray God, in the bowels of his mercy, to send you his Holy Spirit; for he hath given you his great gift of utterance, if it pleased him also to open the eyes of your heart'.[7]

Jane seems, in fact, to have been rather disturbed by the

realisation that she had come dangerously close to liking a Catholic priest; that she had found him sympathetic, intelligent and cultivated – rather more so than some of the Protestants she had known. In the circumstances it was perhaps just as well that she had so little time to brood over the worrying implications of this discovery, which seem to be hinted at in the prayer she is said to have composed shortly before her execution:

O merciful God . . . be thou now unto me a strong tower of defence. . . . Suffer me not to be tempted above my power, but either be thou a deliverer unto me out of this great misery, or else give me grace patiently to bear thy heavy hand and sharp correction. . . . How long wilt thou be absent? – for ever? Oh, Lord! hast thou forgotten to be gracious, and hast thou shut up thy loving kindness in displeasure? Wilt thou be no more entreated? . . . Shall I despair of thy mercy? Oh God! far be that from me. I am thy workmanship, created in Christ Jesus; give me grace therefore to tarry thy leisure and patiently to bear thy works, assuredly knowing, that as thou canst, so thou wilt deliver me when it shall please thee . . . for thou knowest better what is good for me than I do. Therefore do with me in all things what thou wilt. . . . Only, in the meantime, arm me, I beseech thee, with thy armour, that I may stand fast . . . above all things taking to me the shield of faith, wherewith I may be able to quench all the fiery darts of the wicked.[8]

The sharp correction was now no longer to be delayed and those last days were taken up with the macabre preparations which had to be made by all high-born victims of judicial execution. The Lady Jane must choose a suitable dress for her final public appearance and nominate two members of her little household to witness her death and afterwards 'decently dispose' of her body. The speech which she would make from the scaffold must be polished and copied out for subsequent circulation and publication. Then there were farewell letters to be written and farewell gifts chosen. Her sister Katherine was to have her Greek testament – 'it will teach you to live and learn you to die' – plus a long, windy letter of spiritual exhortation, wasted on feather-brained Katherine. To her father, who, together with his brother John, had been brought back to the Tower on Saturday 10 February, she tried to send a message of comfort, though her outraged sense of justice impelled her to remind him that it had pleased God to hasten her death 'by you, by whom my life should rather have been lengthened'. And, she went on,

> albeit I am very well assured of your impatient dolours, redoubled many ways, both in bewailing your own woe, and especially, as I am informed, my woeful estate; yet my dear father . . . herein I may account myself blessed, that washing my hands with the innocence of my fact, my guiltless blood may cry before the Lord, mercy to the innocent! And though I must needs acknowledge, that being constrained, and as you know well enough continually assayed, yet in taking [the crown] upon me, I seemed to consent, and therein grievously offended the queen and her laws, yet do I assuredly trust that this my offence towards God is so much the less, in that being in so royal estate as I was, my enforced honour never mingled with mine innocent heart. And thus, good father, I have opened unto to you the state wherein I presently stand, my death at hand, although to you perhaps it may seem woeful, yet to me there is nothing that can be more welcome than from this vale of misery to aspire to that heavenly throne of all joy and pleasure with Christ my Saviour.[9]

Jane also wrote a shorter, simpler message to her father in the prayer book which she carried with her to the scaffold: 'The Lord comfort your grace, and that in his word wherein all creatures only are to be comforted. And though it hath pleased God to take away two of your children: yet think not, I most humbly beseech your grace, that you have lost them; but trust that we, by leaving this mortal life, have won an immortal life. And I, for my part, as I have honoured your grace in this life, will pray for you in another life.'[10] There is no record of any letter or message for her mother and none for her husband, although Guildford had also written a little note to Suffolk in the margin of Jane's prayer book, wishing him 'long life in this world . . . and in the world to come joy everlasting' from his 'loving and obedient son'.[11]

The story is told that Guildford had expressed a wish to see Jane once more before they died. This was repeated to the queen, who sent word that if it would be any consolation to them the young couple were to be allowed to meet to say goodbye, but Jane refused the proffered indulgence, saying it would only be upsetting and would disturb their 'holy tranquillity' – rather wait until they met again 'in a better place'. She may have hoped that she would like him better there, but the story has the same odour of sanctimonious sentimentality which hangs over most of the anecdotes which have gathered around Jane, and there seems to be no real evidence that she ever showed the slightest interest in Guildford at any time during their imprisonment, or he in her. Much has been made of the fact that the name 'Jane' was carved on a wall of the prison quarters shared by the Dudley brothers, but there is no proof that this was a testimony to anything other than boredom, and no proof that it was even Guildford's work or referred to Jane Grey – the duchess of Northumberland was also called Jane.

However, when the unlucky Guildford was brought out of the Beauchamp Tower at ten o'clock on the morning of

Monday 12 February on his way to the execution ground on Tower Hill, Jane had stationed herself at her window to see his procession leave. She waited obstinately for its return and presently the cart, containing the decapitated carcase of the tall, strong boy who had wanted her to make him king, lying on the bloodstained straw, the head wrapped roughly in a cloth, rattled past below her on its way to the Tower chapel. The sight moved her perhaps more than she had expected, and it is said that those standing by heard her murmur Guildford's name and something about 'the bitterness of death'.

Guildford Dudley had cried like the child he still was when told of his impending fate, but he died like a gentleman, quietly and without fuss, and now it was Jane's turn. Her execution, as befitted a princess of the blood royal, was to take place privately on Tower Green – from Partridge's house she would have had an excellent view of her scaffold being erected 'over against the White Tower' – and as soon as the officials were ready she came out, leaning on the arm of the Lieutenant, Sir John Brydges. Her two attendants, Mrs Ellen and Elizabeth Tylney, were in tears, but Jane herself, wearing the same black gown she had worn to her trial, appeared dry-eyed and perfectly composed, her little prayer book open in her free hand. She climbed the steps of the scaffold and then turned, ready to address the small invited audience which had gathered to see justice done.

She did not waste words. She admitted again that she had done wrong in accepting the crown. '"The fact, indeed, against the queen's highness was unlawful, and the consenting thereunto by me; but touching the procurement and desire thereof by me or on my behalf, I do wash my hands in innocency, before God and you good Christian people, this day", and therewith she wrung her hands, in which she had her book.' She went on to ask all those present to bear witness that she died a good Christian woman and that she looked to be saved 'by none other mean, but only by the mercy of God in the merits of the blood of his only son Jesus Christ. . . . And now, good people,' she ended, 'while I am alive, I pray you to assist me with your prayers.' Even in that last dreadful moment she could find the strength to remain true to her stern Protestant faith and steadfastly reject the age-old comfort of prayers for the dead. Kneeling, she turned to John Feckenham, saying: 'Shall I say this psalm?' and then repeated the fifty-first psalm, the Miserere, in English 'in most devout manner' to the end, Feckenham beside her following her in Latin.

Now there were just the final preparations to be gone through. She got to her feet, handed her gloves and handkerchief to Mrs Tylney and her prayer book to John Brydges' brother Thomas, and began to untie the fastenings of her gown. As the executioner, that nightmare masked figure, stepped forward, Jane, not understanding perhaps that his victim's outer garments were the hangman's traditional perquisite, shrank back and 'desired him to let her alone'. Nurse Ellen and Elizabeth Tylney helped her to take off her dress and gave her a 'fair handkercher to knit about her eyes'. Now the hangman was kneeling for the ritual asking and receiving of forgiveness. He told her to stand upon the straw, and in so doing she saw the block for the first time. There was nothing left to do but make an end. Whispering, 'I pray you dispatch me quickly', she tied the blindfold over her eyes. The world vanished and she was alone, groping in the darkness, crying shockingly, 'What shall I do? Where is it?' Someone stepped forward to guide her, and 'she laid her head down upon the block, and stretched forth her body and said "Lord, into thy hands I commend my spirit!"'[12] The axe swung and blood spouted obscenely over the scaffold, soaking the straw and spattering the standers-by.

The Tower officials, their work done, began to disperse. Perhaps John Brydges was already reading the message Jane had written for him on the flyleaf of her prayer book:

Forasmuch as you have desired so simple a woman to write in so worthy a book, good Master Lieutenant, therefore shall I as a friend desire you, and as a Christian require you, to call upon God, to incline your heart to his laws, to quicken you in his way, and not to take the word of truth utterly out of your mouth. Live still to die, that by death you may purchase eternal life. . . . For, as the preacher sayeth, there is a time to be born and a time to die; and the day of death is better than the day of our birth.

Yours, as the Lord knoweth, as a friend, Jane Duddeley.[13]

There seems to be some doubt as to the details of Jane's burial and a tradition persisted that she had somehow been spirited away to Bradgate, but François de Noailles, the younger brother of Antoine, who arrived in London on 12 February, records having seen her half-naked corpse still lying on the scaffold later that day and commented on the extraordinary amount of blood which had issued from so small a body.[14] The delay in moving the body was probably due more to uncertainty or reluctance on the part of anyone in authority to take responsibility for making the necessary arrangements than to deliberate disrespect and there seems no reason to doubt that some time before nightfall on that Monday the butchered remains of Henry VIII's great-niece were interred beneath the stones of St Peter ad Vincula overlooking Tower Green, there to lie between the bones of two headless queens, Anne Boleyn and Katherine Howard.

The judicial murder of Jane Grey – for no one ever pretended it was anything else – must surely count as one of the most coldly horrifying episodes in English history, but it created no great stir at the time, even among the aggressively Protestant Londoners. Public opinion, which was to play such a significant part in saving the life of her cousin Elizabeth, was not mobilised to help Jane, whose name, so far as it was remembered at all, remained too closely associated with the unpopular Dudleys and their failed coup to rouse much sympathy. There is a tradition that the oak trees in Bradgate Park were pollarded in a gesture of mourning and defiance when news of Lady Jane's beheading reached Leicestershire, and John Foxe preserves the story that Richard Morgan, the judge who had sentenced her, died six months later in a raving delirium, crying: 'Take the Lady Jane from me! Take away the Lady Jane!'[15]

Roger Ascham remembered her, of course. So did John Aylmer, who rose to become bishop of London under Queen Elizabeth, and so perhaps did John Feckenham, who was to spend most of the rest of his long life in prison for his religious beliefs, dying in the concentration camp for Catholic priests at Wisbech in Cam-bridgeshire in 1585, almost the last survivor of his generation. Ironically enough, the most generous tribute paid to Jane at the time of her death came from Monsignor Giovanni Francesco Commendone, who had been sent by the Pope to report on the situation in England and who said of her that 'the girl, born to a misery beyond tears, had faced death with far greater gallantry than it might be expected from her sex and the natural weakness of her age'.[16] John Foxe included her in his gallery of Protestant martyrs, and a somewhat perfunctory regret for the 'casting away' of a fair lady whom both God and nature had endowed with so many singular gifts and graces is expressed in the contemporary histories. In general though, for reasons both personal and political, it became increasingly tactless to mention the Suffolk family in polite Elizabethan circles.

The eighteenth and nineteenth centuries resurrected, canonised and dehumanised Jane Grey, so that the cool, sceptical early twentieth century found her totally incomprehensible. The later twentieth and early twenty-first centuries should have no such difficulty, having become rather better acquainted with the effects of ideological commitment upon personality, for it is only in terms of total commitment to an ideology that Jane can be understood. Only thus is it possible to recognise the loving, lively, gifted child, consistently starved of natural affection, sublimating all her overflowing urges and energies in devotion to an ideal. Jane, in fact, had all the makings of a true fanatic. In another age she would have been the perfect prototype of the partisan, the resistance or freedom fighter, perfectly prepared to sacrifice her own or anyone else's life in the furtherance of some cause, be it religious or political.

On Sunday 11 February 1554 Stephen Gardiner had preached a sermon before Mary in which he asked a boon of the queen's highness that 'like as she had before time extended her mercy' with the result that through her gentleness conspiracy and rebellion had grown, 'she would now be merciful to the body of the commonwealth, and conservation thereof, which could not be unless the rotten and hurtful members were cut off and consumed'.[17] On the following morning, as Jane and Guildford Dudley went to their deaths, gallows were being erected all over London, in the suburbs of Bermondsey and Southwark, in Cheapside and Fleet Street, Smithfield and Holborn, Tower Hill and Leadenhall, and as far west as Charing Cross and Hyde Park Corner. On the 14th the hangings began and soon all the city gates were decorated with severed heads and dismembered corpses in an intentionally grim reminder of the consequences of unsuccessful rebellion. The obliteration of the whole house of Suffolk was also now proceeding to what Simon Renard still regarded as its long-overdue conclusion, and on Saturday 17 February Henry, duke of Suffolk, was taken by river from the Tower to Westminster for his trial, who 'at his going out went out very stoutly and cheerfully enough' but returned 'with a countenance very heavy and pensive, desiring all men to pray for him'.

Suffolk, whose only excuse for his erratic behaviour

apparently was that he had felt himself slighted by the Council since the Northumberland affair, had told his judges that he thought it no treason 'for a peer of the realm as he was to raise his power and make proclamation only to avoid strangers out of the realm'. This might have been a good point, but he spoilt it by going on to boast that he had resisted the queen's lieutenant in the person of the earl of Huntingdon and by these words 'confessed himself guilty of treason'. He also rather unsportingly tried to blame his brother Thomas for having persuaded him to seek sanctuary in Leicestershire, saying that 'it was to be feared he should be put again in the Tower', but 'being in his own country, and amongst friends and tenants, who durst fetch him?' As he went on to admit that he had once said 'at his table over his supper that he would undertake, for need, only with a hundred gentlemen, to set the crown upon Courtenay's head', it is hardly surprising that he should have been convicted and condemned.[18]

'A man of high nobility by birth', pronounced Holinshed's *Chronicle*, 'and of nature to his friends gentle and courteous, more easy indeed to be led than was thought expedient, of stomach nevertheless stout and hardy, hasty and soon kindled but pacified straight again . . . upright and plain in his private dealings.'[19] But in public dealings he was shifty and deceitful, with an unerring instinct for picking the losing side. A weak man, irascible and unstable, and possessing the soul of a petty crook, Henry Grey paid the usual forfeit to the executioner on Tower Hill on Friday 23 February. Like his daughter, he was attended on the scaffold by a Catholic priest, but he died, so he assured the spectators, 'in the faith of Christ, trusting to be saved by his blood only and by none other trumpery'. Holinshed also records that, at the last moment, someone in the crowd called out: 'My lord, how shall I do for the money that you do owe me?' And the duke said, 'Alas, good fellow, I pray thee trouble me not now, but go thy way to my officers.'

Then he repeated the Lord's Prayer and laid down his head on the block. 'And the executioner took the axe and at the first chop stroke off his head, and held it up to the people, according to the common custom.'[20] History does not relate whether the man in the crowd got his money.

Thomas Grey, who had been picked up at Oswestry near the Welsh border as he tried to make his way to the coast, was executed towards the end of April and was among the last of the Wyatt conspirators to suffer. By that time the queen was beginning to issue pardons to convicted rebels and London juries were beginning to return 'not guilty' verdicts. Lord John Grey, although tried and 'cast' as a traitor, was later pardoned and released, as were the surviving Dudley brothers. Edward Courtenay and the Princess Elizabeth also escaped with their lives – much to the irritation of Simon Renard, who did not hesitate to express his opinion that the queen had wasted a heaven-sent opportunity to rid herself of these two so obviously dangerous enemies of the state.

By May the prisons were emptying. Edward Courtenay was consigned to a period of house arrest at Fotheringhay Castle, whence he would presently be sent to travel abroad and would find his death from fever in Italy. Elizabeth, after her brief but well-publicised imprisonment in the Tower, was also dispatched to languish in a remote country house – the old royal hunting lodge at Woodstock in Oxfordshire – while Mary left for Richmond Palace to prepare for her wedding, which was expected to take place some time before the end of June. Gradually the rotting corpses and other depressing reminders of the winter of discontent were being tidied out of sight. It looked like the end of a chapter, and in Strasburg and Zurich there was mourning. 'I hear nothing else from England, except that everything is getting worse and worse,' wrote Peter Martyr to Henry Bullinger on 3 April. 'Jane, who was formerly queen, conducted herself at her execution with the greatest fortitude and godliness, as did also her father and her husband. God be thanked that they persevered in the confession of the true faith!'[21] Another correspondent, writing from London that spring, bewailed the overthrow and near extinction of the very noble family of Grey 'on account of their saving profession of our Saviour, and the cause of the gospel'. Yet, he went on, 'all godly and truly Christian persons have not so much reason to mourn over the ruin of a family so illustrious, as to rejoice that the latest action of her [Jane's] life was terminated in bearing testimony to the name of Jesus; and the rather because those who rest with Christ in the kingdom of his father will not have to behold with their own eyes the wretched and lamentable overthrow of our nation'.[22]

The dukedom of Suffolk was now once more extinct, but it was not quite the end of the story. The widowed duchess consoled herself with even greater rapidity than once her father had done. Apparently undismayed by the violent deaths of her daughter, son-in-law, husband and brother-in-law, within a matter of weeks she had married again – to young Master Adrian Stokes, who is variously described as having been her groom of the chambers, steward or master of the horse. Adrian Stokes may possibly have been the son of John Stokes, the queen's brewer, who supplied the Suffolks with wine and beer, but otherwise there seems to be little or no information about him, except that he was fifteen years younger than his bride, red-haired and with a flashy taste in dress. All the eighteenth- and nineteenth-century commentators were scathing about the match, both because of its unseemly haste and because of the social class of the bridegroom. Plainly the duchess had married beneath her, but it does not follow that Stokes was a mere illiterate yokel. On the contrary, there is some evidence to suggest that he was an educated man. Most likely he was one of those aspiring gentleman servants who swarmed in every great household; eager, resourceful young men drawn from the ranks of the rising professional and merchant classes who were looking for an opportunity to carve out a career in the service of an influential patron. In a society which saw nothing demeaning in the concept of personal service, this was a perfectly acceptable and well-recognised, if chancy, method of getting one's start in life.

Frances Grey was following a family tradition by marrying into a lower social stratum, but in her case there may also have been an element of self-preservation. She was now, after all, in a potentially quite dangerously exposed position: very close to the throne and an eligible widow (she was still only thirty-six) she might well find herself being used, just as her daughter had been, by some group of disaffected Protestants. The acquisition of such an obviously plebeian husband would offer some safeguard against any unwelcome attentions of that kind. The marriage does not seem to have affected her relationship with the queen. Frances continued to be in high favour at court and Mary was going out of her way to be kind to Katherine and Mary, perhaps in an attempt to make up for executing their father and sister. Frances gave birth to another child in November, eight-and-a-half months after her second marriage, but the infant, a girl, died the same day. Sad Mary Tudor died unlamented in November 1558 to be succeeded by the half-sister she had so bitterly resented. Frances was to die the following October after a long illness and 'out of the great affection she bore the duchess and because of her kinship' the new Queen Elizabeth gave her a royal funeral in Westminster Abbey. 'The most noble and excellent princess, the Lady Frances, late Duchess of Suffolk' was laid to rest in St Edmund's Chapel under a pompous alabaster monument, paid for by Adrian Stokes – a stark contrast to that unmarked dishonoured grave under the stones in St Peter-ad-Vincula by Tower Green.

Katherine and Mary, now aged nineteen and fourteen, were still at court and still unspoken for – and their future, especially Katherine's, was the subject of a good deal of speculation. If the controversial provisions of Henry VIII's will were to be followed, Katherine had now inherited the position of heir presumptive and as such had become a figure of international political importance, but unhappily she possessed none of the qualities of tact, discretion or even basic common sense which might have helped her to survive in the political jungle. To make matters worse, she did not get on with the queen, telling the Spanish ambassador that she experienced 'nothing but discourtesy' from her cousin.

The fact that Elizabeth and Katherine Grey were on bad terms was soon being noticed in certain circles and during the second half of 1559 Thomas Challoner, the English ambassador in Brussels, warned the queen about rumours that the Spaniards were planning to kidnap Lady Katherine. Apparently the idea was to marry her to Don Carlos, Philip's imbecile son, or 'with some other person of less degree if less depended on her', and then keep her as a possible counter-claimant to France's Mary Queen of Scots should the occasion arise. Since Katherine was known to be of 'discontented mind' and not regarded or esteemed by the queen, it was thought there would be no difficulty in enticing her away.[23]

In fact, it is unlikely that Katherine even knew about any of these conjectural Spanish intrigues or that she took any interest in the ramifications of European politics. In 1559 she was interested only in her own plans to marry Edward Seymour, earl of Hertford, the same who had once been suggested as a bridegroom for her sister Jane. She would, of course, have known him since childhood, but it was during Queen Mary's reign, when Katherine had been staying with the duchess of Somerset at Hanworth, that the two young people had first begun 'to accompany together' and to think about marriage. The idea of the match had been discussed in the Seymour and Grey families in the spring of 1559 and Katherine's mother had agreed to approach the queen for her consent. But unfortunately the approach was never made. Frances became seriously ill in the summer and by November she was dead. The lovers now had no influential person to speak for them and the whole affair might well have died a natural death had not Hertford's sister, Lady Jane Seymour, decided to take a hand.

Jane Seymour was one of Katherine's fellow maids of honour, an ambitious and forceful young woman, determined that her brother should not lose the chance of making such a brilliant match. It was Jane who brought the couple together again – they had quarrelled when Hertford began to pay attention to another, quite inferior girl – and it was almost certainly she who put the disastrous idea of a secret marriage into their heads. The three of them met in Lady Jane's private closet at Whitehall some time in October 1560 and there Katherine and Edward Seymour plighted their troth. It was agreed that the wedding should take place at the earl's house in Canon Row 'the next time that the queen's highness should take any journey' and Jane undertook to have a clergyman standing by.

Opportunity came early in December when the queen decided to go down to Eltham for a few days' hunting. Katherine pleaded toothache and Jane, who was already consumptive, was often ailing. As soon as Elizabeth was safely out of the way, the two girls slipped out of the palace and walked along the sands by the river to Canon Row. The marriage ceremony was performed in Hertford's bedroom and afterwards, while Lady Jane kept guard in the next room, the newly married couple went to bed and had 'carnal copulation'. They did not have long together – questions would be asked if Katherine failed to appear at dinner with the Controller of the Household – and after about an hour and a half they had to start scrambling back into their clothes.

Katherine might have achieved her immediate ambition, but her altered status made little practical difference to her circumstances. She and Hertford still had to be content with furtive meetings at Whitehall, Greenwich or Canon Row, odd hours snatched whenever they could manage it. How long they expected to keep their secret is impossible to say. Neither of them appears to have given any serious thought to the question of how they were going to break the news, but it was not long before events began to catch up with them. Jane Seymour died in March 1561 and without her help it was more difficult for them to meet. Then the queen decided to send the earl of Hertford abroad as a companion to William Cecil's son, who was going to France to finish his education. This was an unexpected complication, to be followed by another, not so unexpected. Katherine thought she might be pregnant, but could not or would not say for certain. Her husband went abroad in April, probably rather relieved to escape, at least temporarily, from a situation that was rapidly getting out of hand, but promising to return if she wrote to tell him she was definitely with child.

Left alone, Katherine seems at last to have begun to realise the enormity of what she had done. The fact of her pregnancy could no longer be ignored and already some suspicious glances were being cast at her shape. In July she had to accompany the queen on a progress to East Anglia and at the beginning of August, while the court was at Ipswich, the secret finally came out.

The queen, understandably, was furious. She had never liked Katherine, but considered she had always treated her fairly. Now the girl had repaid her with ingratitude, deceit and perhaps worse. Anything which touched the succession touched Elizabeth on her most sensitive spot. She was never to forget her own experiences as 'a second person' in her sister's reign, and the intrigues which inevitably surrounded an heir presumptive. Now, in the activities of Katherine Grey she had caught a sulphurous whiff of treason. Katherine's choice of husband was also unfortunate. The Seymours had a reputation for political ambition and their connection with the royal family was uncomfortably close. If the young Hertfords were to produce a son, it would complicate still further an already sufficiently complicated dynastic situation. The new countess was therefore promptly committed to the Tower, where the earl soon joined her, and the government's investigators proceeded to extract from them every detail of that hole-and-corner marriage in the house at Canon Row.[24]

On 24 September Katherine duly gave birth to a healthy son, who was christened after his father in the chapel of St Peter ad Vincula, in close proximity to the headless remains of both his grandfathers, two of his great-uncles and his aunt Jane Grey. The most exhaustive enquiries had failed to uncover any evidence of a plot involving the baby's parents – although the queen was still not entirely convinced – and as it was no longer a treasonable offence *per se* for a member of the royal family to marry without the sovereign's consent, Elizabeth was obliged to resort to the expedient of attacking the validity of the marriage. Since the only witness to the ceremony was now dead and the officiating clergyman had vanished without trace, this did not present much difficulty – especially as Katherine was predictably unable to produce the deed of jointure her husband had given her before he left for France. This document, she tearfully informed her interrogators, had been put safely away, but 'with moving from place to place at progress time, it is lost and she cannot tell where it is become'. In short, although the couple agreed 'on the time, place and company of their marriage', they could not produce a scrap of evidence to prove that it had ever taken place. The queen, therefore, put the whole matter in the hands of the ecclesiastical authorities and on 10 May 1562 the archbishop of Canterbury gave judgement that there had been no marriage between the earl of Hertford and Lady Katherine Grey. He censured them both for having committed fornication and recommended a heavy fine and imprisonment during the queen's pleasure.

The culprits remained in the Tower but there were some compensations. The Lieutenant, Sir Edward Warner, was a kindly man. He allowed Katherine to keep her pet dogs and monkeys, in spite of the damage these quite unhousetrained creatures were doing to government property. He also, on occasion, allowed her to see her husband, turning a discreetly blind eye to unlocked doors, and during the summer of 1562 the Hertfords enjoyed the nearest approach to a normal married life they were ever to know. Then, in February 1563 came the inevitable sequel – Katherine had another baby, another healthy son.

This time the queen was really angry. She found it very difficult to forgive her cousin for her apparently cynical disregard for the authority and prestige of the Crown; for the fact that instead of showing contrition, or even any understanding of the nature of her crime, she had deliberately gone and done it again. To one of Elizabeth's highly disciplined intelligence and acute political awareness it naturally seemed incredible that Katherine could simply have been following her natural urges rather than acting from premeditated malice or ambition.

The queen's temper and the Hertfords' prospects were not improved by the existence of widespread public sympathy for the young couple. Their romantic story had appealed to the imagination of the Londoners who felt that their inability to prove their marriage was more their misfortune than their fault, and in other parts of the country, too, ignorant folk were not hesitating to say openly that they were man and wife 'and why should man and wife be let from coming together?'[25] This attitude was not shared by the authorities who considered it was high time that the earl was made to realise just what it meant to have 'so arrogantly and contemptuously offended his prince'.

Neither Hertford nor Katherine was to be left in any doubt in future as to what it meant to have offended their prince. (Nor was Edward Warner, who had been summarily sacked from his post and temporarily incarcerated in his own prison.) There were no more unlocked doors or stolen meetings, and a serious outbreak of plague in the capital that summer provided an excuse for separating the little family still more completely. The earl and the elder child were sent to live under house arrest with his mother at Hanworth, while Katherine and the new baby left in the opposite direction, to her surviving uncle Lord John Grey at Pirgo in Essex, with strict instructions that she was to be kept 'as in custody' and not allowed any unsupervised contact with the outside world.

There was no question now about Katherine's contrition. John Grey reported that his erring niece was indeed 'a penitent and sorrowful woman for the queen's displeasure' and Katherine herself wrote to Secretary William Cecil on 3 September, beseeching his help 'for the obtaining of the queen's majesty's most gracious pardon and favour towards me, which with upstretched hands and down bent knees, from the bottom of my heart, most humbly I crave'.[26]

But no immediate signs of either pardon or favour were forthcoming and John Grey was soon writing again to remind Cecil of his promise of friendship and goodwill. The Lady Katherine, it seems, was pining away for the want of the queen's favour. She was eating hardly anything and was permanently dissolved in tears: 'I never came near her but I found her weeping, or else saw by her face that she had wept.' Lord John was, in fact, becoming seriously worried about her health. 'She is so fraughted with phlegm, by reason of thought, weeping and sitting still, that many hours she is like to be overcome therewith.'[27] The wretched Katherine's troubles were aggravated by the fact that she appears to have been virtually destitute. She had no money, no plate and, according to John Grey, was so poorly furnished that he was ashamed to let William Cecil have an inventory of her possessions. Lord John had reluctantly supplied the most glaring deficiencies, but he baulked at paying for his charge's keep and when the queen complained about his expenses he retaliated by sending a detailed account to Cecil. The weekly rate for 'my lady of Hertford's board, her child and her folks' amounted to £6 10s 8d. As this included eight servants and even five shillings to the widow who washed the baby's clothes, it sounds reasonable enough, but Elizabeth, who was never averse to having things both ways, decreed that henceforward the earl of Hertford should be made responsible for Katherine's maintenance and he was ordered to pay the sum of £114 to the Greys.[28]

Elizabeth was not normally vindictive and once she felt satisfied that the Hertfords had thoroughly learned their lesson she might have responded to their frequent tear-stained appeals for mercy – indeed, hints to this effect had already been dropped. Unfortunately, though, in the spring of 1564 John Hales, an official in the Lord Chancellor's department and extreme left-wing MP, which, in the Elizabethan context, meant militant Protestant activist, took it upon himself to publish a *Discourse on the Succession* in which he set out the superior claim of Katherine Grey over that of Mary Queen of Scots to be recognised as heir presumptive. 'This dealing of his', remarked William Cecil (who also privately supported Katherine Grey), 'offendeth the Queen's majesty very much.'[29]

Hales's crime did not merely consist of meddling in matters which were none of his business, or even his support of the Suffolk claim. More to the point was the fact that he had involved other people and had taken active steps to try to establish the legality of the Grey/Seymour alliance, consulting European jurists and procuring from them 'sentences and counsels . . . maintaining the lawfulness of the Earl of Hertford's marriage'. Lady Katherine, an Englishwoman born and bred and boasting an impeccable Protestant background, had always been first choice of heir among the influential Protestant establishment. If a viable case were now made out for the validity of her marriage, then, as the mother of two sons, her claim to be given precedence over the Stuart line would be immensely strengthened. It was not to be supposed that Mary Queen of Scots and her party would let this pass without strong protest, and the whole delicate balance of Anglo-Scottish relations – not to mention England's relations with France and Spain – would be endangered at a time when international tension caused by the ideological Catholic versus Protestant conflict was being steadily heightened. Vexed beyond measure, Elizabeth clapped the officious Mr Hales into prison and ordered a full enquiry. She was not in the least appeased by his agitated assurances that his only thought had been to promote the Protestant Tudor line against the Catholic Mary Stuart. The succession was a matter which the queen regarded as being entirely within her own prerogative and over which she would not tolerate outside interference on any pretext.

The dust raised by the Hales affair subsided slowly and Hales himself was released, but Katherine Grey remained under arrest. John Grey died in the autumn of 1564 and Katherine was transferred to the custody of Sir William Petre of Ingatestone, her prospects of ever being reunited with her 'dear lord and husband' looking as remote as ever. Then, in the summer of 1565, an element of black comedy entered the story of the Grey sisters.

'Here is an unhappy chance and monstrous,' wrote William Cecil to his friend Thomas Smith on 21 August. 'The Sergeant Porter, being the biggest gentleman in this court, hath married secretly the Lady Mary Grey, the least of all the court. They are committed to several [separate] prisons. The offence is very great.'[30] The current Spanish ambassador, Guzman da Silva, thought it worth while to pass on the news to King Philip, explaining that the queen had in her house a sister of Jane and Katherine Grey. 'She is little, crook-backed and very ugly, and it came out yesterday that she had married a gentleman named Keys, sergeant porter at the palace. They say', he added ominously, 'the Queen is very much annoyed and grieved thereat.'[31]

Little enough seems to be known about the background to this bizarre romance between the enormous gatekeeper, a middle-aged widower with several children, and the dwarfish nineteen-year-old Mary Grey. As a child, Mary had been briefly betrothed to her kinsman Arthur Grey of Wilton, but no other attempt had ever been made to arrange a marriage for her, and since Katherine's disgrace it was obvious that none ever would be. Mary, who seems to have shared some, at least, of Jane's intellectual interests as well as her stubborn independence of spirit, had therefore decided to make her own arrangements, apparently undeterred by the example of Katherine's disastrous experience. Her attachment to Thomas Keys (whose name most probably derived from his office) is said to have begun about a year before their marriage which, as in the case of the late Lady Frances, was not quite so unequal as at first appeared, Keys being related to the highly respectable and royally connected Knollys family.

The actual wedding had taken place at nine o'clock at night on either 10 or 12 August in the porter's rooms over the Watergate at Whitehall. As in the case of Katherine and Edward Seymour, the officiating clergyman, described as an old man, short and very fat, failed to leave his name and address, but there were a sufficient number of witnesses present able to testify that the ceremony had actually been performed. This time, though, the authorities were not taking any risks. The unfortunate Thomas Keys was incarcerated in the Fleet prison while Mary Grey was removed to a safe distance – to Chequers in Buckinghamshire and the custody of William Hawtrey Esquire, the first of a succession of unwilling gaoler hosts. As with Katherine, Mary appears to have been virtually destitute of both money and possessions, having nothing but an old feather bed, 'all torn and full of patches, without either bolster or counterpane . . . an old quilt of silk, so tattered as the cotton of it comes out' and 'two little pieces of old hangings, both of them not seven yards broad'. Like Katherine, Mary pined. According to Charles Brandon's widow, the second duchess of Suffolk, now also remarried to a member of her household staff and to whose custody Mary was transferred in 1567, 'all she has eaten these two days is not so much as a chicken's leg'.[32] Like Katherine, too, she addressed repeated and equally unavailing tear-stained appeals for forgiveness.

Katherine, though, was writing no more letters and showing no sign of interest in the outside world. She had, it seemed, long since given up all hope of pardon or release, much less of ever seeing her husband again. In February 1567 she was living at Gosfield Hall near Halstead in Essex, in the charge of Sir John Wentworth, and in September was moved again, to Cockfield Hall, home of Sir Owen Hopton and his wife, in the remote Suffolk village of Yoxford. She was by this time in the terminal stages of tuberculosis, and soon after her arrival Sir Owen was obliged to send for one of the royal physicians to visit her. But there was nothing left for Katherine now except to die as becomingly, if less dramatically, as her sister Jane had done, and in January 1568 Owen Hopton wrote to inform William Cecil that the end was not far off.

It came on the morning of the 27th. Between six and seven o'clock she sent for Owen Hopton and begged him, and the others present, to bear witness that she died a true Christian, that she believed herself to be saved by the death of Christ and was one that he had shed his precious blood for. Katherine then begged Hopton that he would himself ask the queen, 'even from the mouth of a dead woman', that she would at last 'forgive her displeasure towards me' and went on to plead that Elizabeth would be good to her children and 'not impute my fault unto them, whom I give wholly unto her majesty'. Finally there were 'certain commendations and tokens' for her husband: the ring with a pointed diamond which he had given her when they plighted their troth in Jane Seymour's closet in the Maidens' Chamber at Westminster seven years before, her wedding ring and another ring engraved with a death's head and the motto 'While I live yours'. She asked Hertford that as she had been a true and faithful wife, he would be a loving and natural father to their children and she sent her little sons her blessing. Owen Hopton, 'perceiving her to draw towards her end', gave orders for the passing bell to be rung and Katherine Seymour, born Katherine Grey, 'yielded unto God her meek spirit at nine of the clock in the morning', having given, at least according to the official account, the smoothly polished performance expected of persons of breeding and education as they stood on the brink of eternity.[33] Katherine's last moments, if less publicly impressive than those of her elder sister, seem to have been no less dignified or, in their own way, tragic. She was twenty-seven years old. She had spent the last six-and-a-half years in prison or under house arrest – and the whole of her life under the doom of her royal blood.

For the earl of Hertford his wife's death brought new hope of release and rehabilitation. He was then living comfortably enough with Sir John Spencer at Althorp but had to wait another two years before his freedom of movement was finally restored. He remained faithful to Katherine's memory for nearly twenty years, eventually remarrying to a daughter of the powerful Howard clan, but he never gave up the fight to get his first marriage recognised and his sons' legitimacy established. At last, in 1606, three years after the old queen's death, perseverance was rewarded when the priest who had performed the ceremony at Canon Row half a century before was suddenly and miraculously resurrected. The earl lived on until 1621 and was to see his grandson re-enact his own story with almost uncanny precision by making a runaway marriage with Lady Arbella Stuart, another junior member of the royal house.

Mary Grey was finally released some time in 1572, about a year after the death of her husband. She herself died in poverty and obscurity in the early summer of 1578. Lady Mary would have been thirty-two years old and with her death vanished almost the last remnant of the once-great House of Suffolk. But outcast though she had become, under the terms of her great-uncle's infamous will, Mary Keys, widow, of the parish of St Botolph's without Aldersgate, died heiress presumptive to the crown of England – that deadly legacy which had so poisoned the lives of the descendants of Mary Brandon, born Mary Tudor.

The only surviving representative of the junior branch of the Suffolk line, Eleanor Brandon's daughter Margaret, married Henry Stanley, Lord Strange, in 1555 and became countess of Derby and queen in Man when her husband succeeded to the title in 1572. Her life, blighted by ill-health and family quarrels, was not a happy one, but she did at least avoid the worst of the calamities that befell her Grey cousins. In spite of chronic rheumatism and toothache, her husband's infidelities and their acrimonious financial disputes, the countess of Derby raised a family of four sons and one daughter and lived on into the mid-1590s. She seems to have been rather a silly woman, the historian William Camden saying of her that 'through an idle mixture of curiosity and ambition, supported by sanguine hopes and a credulous fancy, she much used the conversations of necromancers and figure flingers'.[34] An interest in the occult, although widespread among Elizabethans, could be a dangerous hobby; an interest in fortune-telling especially so for one in Margaret's position on the periphery of the succession dispute, and on one occasion it earned her the queen's serious displeasure and a spell of imprisonment.

Her eldest son Ferdinando, Lord Strange, courtier, man

of letters, friend and patron of poets and poet in a small way himself, stood out as a colourful and slightly sinister figure on the Elizabethan scene. He is best remembered for his interest in the theatre – Lord Strange's men were among the foremost acting companies in the profession. When he succeeded his father, one of the richest peers in the country, in 1593, he became briefly the target of a more than usually optimistic Catholic plot which sought to exploit his 'propinquity of blood' to the royal house. But although well known for their Catholic sympathies, the earls of Derby had always remained conspicuously loyal and Ferdinando wasted no time in informing the government of the approaches being made to him.

As always in the story of sixteenth-century England, so much comes back to the fatal Tudor inability to produce sons and asks so many 'what ifs'. What if Henry VIII's first wife had been able to give him a male heir? What if Edward VI had survived to perpetuate his line? But most poignant of all must be what if Jane Grey had lived? How would she have developed and how might she have influenced the history of her times? Whether we should today regard her 'attainments in literature' with quite such awe as her contemporary admirers is perhaps questionable. Her education was after the fashion of her times narrowly classical and would not have included any English or modern European history, geography or, of course, anything even faintly scientific. One thing, though, seems certain – Jane, alone among her Tudor cousins, was a true scholar who loved learning for its own sake and not as a means to an end. Could she, at any stage, have avoided her destiny? It seems unlikely, given the pressure exerted upon her. Or was she in some sense a willing victim, believing God must have chosen her as his instrument to maintain the true religion?

Let Jane have the last word, in the lines she had written in Latin and Greek on the last page of the prayer book she carried with her to the scaffold: 'Death will give pain to my body for its sins, but the soul will be justified before God.' And in English: 'If my faults deserve punishment, my youth at least and my imprudence were worthy of excuse. God and posterity will show me favour.'[35]

# Genealogical Table

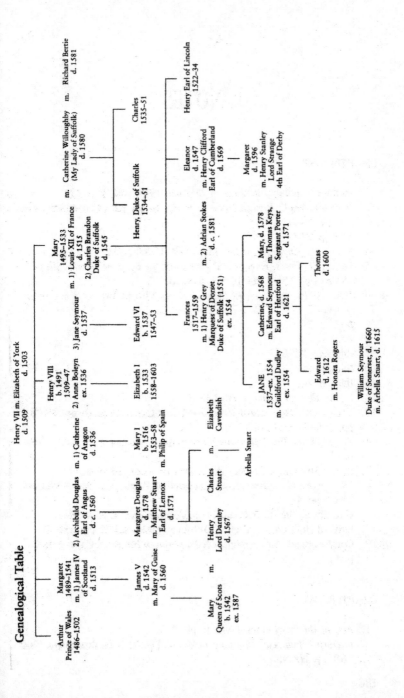

# NOTES

CHAPTER ONE

1. William Dugdale, *Baronage of England*, 1716, vol. 1, p. 721.
2. *Polydore Vergil's English History*, ed. Sir Henry Ellis, Camden Society, no. 29, 1844, p. 203.
3. Ibid., p. 214.
4. S.J. Gunn, *Charles Brandon*, Blackwell, 1988, p. 28.
5. *Letters & Papers, Foreign & Domestic, of the Reign of Henry VIII*, ed. J.S. Brewer, 1862, vol. II, pt i, p. xxxii.
6. *Letters & Papers . . . of the Reign of Henry VIII*, ed. Brewer, vol. I, pt ii, p. 1422.
7. Ibid., p. 76.
8. Ibid., p. 73.
9. Ibid., pp. 74–5.
10. Ibid., p. 75.
11. Ibid., p. xxv.
12. Gunn, *Charles Brandon*, pp. 131–2.
13. W.C. Richardson, *Mary Tudor, The White Queen*, Peter Owen, 1970, pp. 259–61 and 266.
14. C.V. Malfatti, *Two Italian Accounts of Tudor England*, Barcelona, 1953, p. 37.
15. Agnes Strickland, *Lives of the Tudor Princesses*, 1868, p. 96.
16. *Luis Vives and the Renascence Education of Women*, ed. Foster Watson, 1912, pp. 41–2.
17. G.R. Elton, *The Tudor Constitution*, Cambridge, 1972, p. 391.
18. Edward Hall, *Chronicle*, ed. C. Whibley, 1904, vol. II, pp. 356–7.
19. Conyers Read, *Mr Secretary Cecil and Queen Elizabeth*, Cape, 1965, p. 41.


CHAPTER TWO

1. *Acts of the Privy Council*, vol. II, pp. 4–5.
2. *Literary Remains of King Edward VI*, ed. J.G. Nichols, Roxburghe Club, 1857, p. lxxxvii.

3. Ibid., p. xcv.
4. *Luis Vives and the Renascence Education of Women*, ed. Watson, p. 133.
5. Agnes Strickland, *Lives of the Queens of England*, 1844, vol. V, p. 90.
6. Sir John Hayward, *The Life and Reign of King Edward VI*, 1630, p. 196.
7. *Letters & Papers . . . of the Reign of Henry VIII*, ed. Brewer, vol. XXI, pt ii, p. 634.
8. *Collection of State Papers . . . left by William Cecil, Lord Burghley*, ed. Samuel Haynes, 1740, p. 83.
9. P.F. Tytler, *England Under the Reigns of Edward VI and Mary*, 1839, vol. I, pp. 137–8.
10. *Lamentation of a Sinner*, cited in Susan James, *Kateryn Parr*, Ashgate Publishing Ltd, 1999, pp. 199–200.
11. *Luis Vives and the Renascence Education of Women*, ed. Watson, pp. 43–4.
12. *Burghley State Papers*, ed. Haynes, p. 99.
13. Hayward, *The Life and Reign of King Edward VI*, 1630, p. 197.
14. Tytler, *England under the Reigns of Edward VI and Mary*, p. 149; *Burghley State Papers*, ed. Haynes, pp. 75–6.
15. W.K. Jordan, *Edward VI: The Young King*, Allen & Unwin, 1968, p. 380; Jennifer Loach, *Edward VI*, Yale University Press, 1999, p. 57.
16. *Burghley State Papers*, ed. Haynes, pp. 99–100.
17. Ibid., p. 96.
18. Henry Clifford, *Life of Jane Dormer*, ed. J. Stevenson, 1887, p. 86.
19. *Syllogue Epistolarum*, ed. T. Hearne, Oxford, 1716, pp. 151 and 165–6.
20. Tytler, *England under the Reigns of Edward VI and Mary*, p. 123.
21. *Burghley State Papers*, ed. Haynes, pp. 103–4.
22. Ibid., pp. 77–8.
23. Ibid., p. 78.
24. Ibid., p. 93.
25. Tytler, *England under the Reigns of Edward VI and Mary*, p. 139; *Burghley State Papers*, ed. Haynes, p. 76.
26. Tytler, *England under the Reigns of Edward VI and Mary*, p. 133.
27. Ibid., p. 140.
28. *Burghley State Papers*, ed. Haynes, pp. 81–2.
29. Ibid., p. 80.
30. Tytler, *England under the Reigns of Edward VI and Mary*, pp. 144–5.
31. *Burghley State Papers*, ed. Haynes, pp. 97–9.
32. Ibid., p. 94.
33. *Acts of the Privy Council*, vol. II, pp. 246–7 and 262.
34. *Sermons of Hugh Latimer*, ed. John Watkins, 1926, vol. I,

pp. 161–2; J. Strype, *Ecclesiastical Memorials*, 1822, vol. II, pt I, p. 199.

35. James, *Kateryn Parr*, pp. 338–9.
36. Holinshed's *Chronicle*, 1807, vol. III, p. 1014.


CHAPTER THREE


1. Roger Ascham, *The Scholemaster*, ed. J. Mayor, 1863, pp. 33–4.
2. *Original Letters Relative to the English Reformation (Zurich Letters)*, ed. H. Robinson, vol. I, Parker Society, no. 23, 1846, pp. 282 and 286–7.
3. R. Davey, *The Nine Days' Queen*, Methuen, 1909, pp. 175–6.
4. *Original Letters*, vol. I, pp. 6–7.
5. Ibid., vol. II, p. 432.
6. Ibid., vol. I, p. 280.
7. Ibid., pp. 278–9.
8. Ibid., p. 8.
9. Ibid., pp. 9–11.
10. Ibid., vol. II, p. 430.
11. *Diary of Henry Machyn*, ed. J.G. Nichols, Camden Society, no. 42, 1848, p. 9.
12. *Literary Remains of King Edward VI* (Journal), vol. II, p. 359.
13. Ibid., p. 363.
14. *Cal. S.P. Spanish*, vol. X, p. 212.
15. *Literary Remains of Edward VI*, vol. II, p. 308.
16. *Cal. S.P. Spanish*, vol. X, p. 215.
17. Agnes Strickland, *Elizabeth I*, Everyman edn, pp. 49–50.
18. John Strype, *Life of John Aylmer*, Oxford, 1821, p. 196.
19. Frederick Madden, *Privy Purse Expenses of the Princess Mary*, 1831, p. 199.
20. Strickland, *Lives of the Tudor Princesses*, p. 126.
21. *Original Letters*, vol. II, pp. 285–6.
22. *Literary Remains of Edward VI*, vol. II, p. 390.
23. *Original Letters*, vol. II, p. 447.
24. John Foxe, *Acts and Monuments*, ed. G. Townsend and S.R. Cattley, 8 vols, 1837, vol. 8, p. 700.
25. *Statutes of the Realm*, Record Commission, vol. IV, pp. 24 *et seq.*
26. Susan Brigden, *London and the Reformation*, Clarendon Press, 1991, p. 437.
27. Charles Wriothesley, *Chronicle of England*, ed. W. Douglas Hamilton, Camden Society, N.S. 20, 1877, vol. II, pp. 83–4.
28. *Cal. S.P. Venetian*, vol. V, pp. 345–8.

29. *Literary Remains of Edward VI*, vol. II, p. 337.
30. Jennifer Loach, *Edward VI*, Yale University Press, 1999, p. 96 note.
31. Hester Chapman, *The Last Tudor King*, Jonathan Cape, 1958, pp. 260–1.
32. *Cal. S.P. Spanish*, vol. IX, pp. 8–9; *Diary of Henry Machyn*, pp. 30–1.
33. *Cal. S.P. Spanish*, vol. IX, p. 10.
34. Ibid., p. 35.
35. Ibid., p. 49.

CHAPTER FOUR

1. Tytler, *England Under the Reigns of Edward VI and Mary*, vol. II, p. 115.
2. Strype, *Ecclesiastical Memorials*, vol. II, pt ii, p. 505.
3. *Cal. S.P. Spanish*, vol. XI, p. 35.
4. Ibid., p. 46.
5. Strickland, *Lives of the Tudor Princesses*, p. 136.
6. Strype, *Ecclesiastical Memorials*, vol. II, pt ii, p. 111.
7. E.H. Harbison, *Rival Ambassadors at the Court of Queen Mary*, Princeton University Press, 1940, p. 36.
8. *Cal. S.P. Spanish*, vol. XI, p. 46.
9. *Literary Remains of Edward VI*, vol. II, p. 571.
10. *Chronicle of Queen Jane*, ed. J.G. Nichols, Camden Society, no. 48, 1850, App. I, p. 93.
11. *Cal. S.P. Spanish*, vol. XI, p. 44.
12. Ibid., p. 54.
13. Hayward, *Life of Edward VI*, cited in *Literary Remains of Edward VI*, vol. I, pp. cxcvii–cxcviii.
14. *Literary Remains of Edward VI*, vol. II, pp. 567–9.
15. Ibid., p. 566.
16. *Cal. S.P. Spanish*, vol. XI, p. 57.
17. Ibid., p. 66.
18. Loach, *Edward VI*, p. 162.
19. J.M. Stone, *The History of Mary I, Queen of England*, 1901, App. C, pp. 496 *et seq*.; Strickland, *Lives of the Tudor Princesses*, pp. 141–5; Davey, *The Nine Days Queen*, pp. 236–7 and 250–2.
20. Cited in Davey, *The Nine Days Queen*, p. 253.
21. Stone, *Mary I*, pp. 498–9; Davey, *The Nine Days Queen*, p. 261; Strickland, *Lives of the Tudor Princesses*, pp. 151–2.
22. *Chronicle of Queen Jane*, App. V, p. 115.
23. *Cal. S.P. Spanish*, vol. XI, pp. 62–5.
24. Ibid., pp. 72–4.

25. Ibid., pp. 75–6; *Chronicle of Queen Jane*, p. 2.
26. Strype, *Ecclesiastical Memorials*, vol. III, pt i, p. 6.
27. *Chronicle of Queen Jane*, App. II, pp. 103–4.
28. Foxe, *Acts and Monuments*, vol. VI, p. 385.
29. *Cal. S.P. Spanish*, vol. XI, pp. 82–3.
30. *Literary Remains of Lady Jane Grey with a Memoir by N.H. Nicolas*, ed. N.H. Nicolas, 1825, pp. xlix–l.
31. George Howard, *Lady Jane Grey and her Times*, 1822, p. 257; Strickland, *Lives of the Tudor Princesses*, p. 155.
32. Harbison, *Rival Ambassadors*, p. 47.
33. *Cal. S.P. Spanish*, vol. XI, pp. 83–6.
34. *Chronicle of Queen Jane*, p. 5.
35. *Diary of Henry Machyn*, p. 34.
36. *Chronicle of Queen Jane*, pp. 5–6.
37. Ibid., pp. 6–7.
38. *Cal. S.P. Spanish*, vol. XI, pp. 88–9.
39. *Chronicle of Queen Jane*, p. 8.
40. Ibid., pp. 8–9.
41. Ibid., p. 9.
42. *Cal. S.P. Spanish*, pp. 95–6.
43. *Chronicle of Queen Jane*, pp. 11–12; *Diary of Henry Machyn*, p. 37; *Wriothesley's Chronicle*, vol. II, pp. 88–9; *Cal. S.P. Spanish*, vol. XI, p. 96.

CHAPTER FIVE

1. *Chronicle of Queen Jane*, p. 12.
2. Strickland, *Lives of the Tudor Princesses*, pp. 166–7.
3. *Chronicle of Queen Jane*, p. 10.
4. *Cal. S.P. Spanish*, vol. IX, pp. 96 and 105.
5. Cited in Harbison, *Rival Ambassadors*, p. 53.
6. Howard, *Lady Jane Grey*, pp. 307–9.
7. *Cal. S.P. Spanish*, vol. IX, pp. 119–21.
8. *Chronicle of Queen Jane*, p. 14; *Wriothesley's Chronicle*, vol. II, p. 93.
9. *Chronicle of Queen Jane*, p. 14.
10. Stone, *Mary I*, App. C, pp. 496–7.
11. *Cal. S.P. Spanish*, vol. IX, pp. 110–11 and 122.
12. Ibid., pp. 168–9.
13. *Chronicle of Queen Jane*, pp. 18–19.
14. Howard, *Lady Jane Grey*, p. 322–3.
15. Ibid., p. 317.
16. *Chronicle of Queen Jane*, pp. 24–6.

17. *Original Letters*, vol. I, p. 290.
18. *Literary Remains of Lady Jane Grey*, p. 22.
19. Ibid., pp. 23–5.
20. Ibid., pp. 33–4.
21. *Cal. S.P. Spanish*, vol. XI, p. 418.
22. Ibid., p. 241.
23. Holinshed's *Chronicle*, vol. IV, p. 10; *Chronicle of Queen Jane*, p. 32.
24. *Cal. S.P. Spanish*, vol. XI, pp. 359 and 366.
25. *Cal. S.P. Spanish*, vol. XI, p. 366.
26. Ibid., pp. 213 and 289.
27. Ibid., p. 312.
28. Ibid., p. 364.
29. Strype, *Ecclesiastical Memorials*, vol. III, pt I, pp. 85–6.
30. *Cal. S.P. Spanish*, vol. IX, pp. 343 and 372.
31. Tytler, *England Under the Reigns of Edward VI and Mary*, vol. II, p. 263.
32. *Cal. S.P. Spanish*, vol. IX, p. 404.
33. F. Mumby, *The Girlhood of Queen Elizabeth*, 1909, p. 97.
34. *Chronicle of Queen Jane*, p. 34.
35. Ibid., p. 35.
36. Cited in Harbison, *Rival Ambassadors*, pp. 126–7.
37. *Chronicle of Queen Jane*, pp. 38–9.
38. Foxe, *Acts and Monuments*, vol. VI, pp. 414–15.
39. *Chronicle of Queen Jane*, p. 43.
40. Ibid., pp. 45–50 and 133 note; *Diary of Henry Machyn*, pp. 53–4; Wriothesley's *Chronicle*, vol. II, pp. 110–11.

CHAPTER SIX

1. *Cal. S.P. Spanish*, vol. XII, p. 86.
2. *Chronicle of Queen Jane*, p. 37.
3. Holinshed's *Chronicle*, vol. IV, pp. 33–4.
4. Ibid., p. 14.
5. Ibid.; *Cal. S.P. Spanish*, vol. XII, p. 85.
6. Strype, *Ecclesiastical Memorials*, vol. III, pt i, p. 141.
7. Foxe, *Acts and Monuments*, vol. VI, pp. 415–17.
8. *Literary Remains of Lady Jane Grey*, pp. 50–1.
9. Ibid., pp. 47–8.
10. Ibid., pp. 57–8.
11. Ibid., p. 57.
12. *Chronicle of Queen Jane*, pp. 54–9.
13. *Literary Remains of Lady Jane Grey*, pp. 58–9.

14. Davey, *The Nine Days Queen*, pp. 345–6; also Harbison, *Rival Ambassadors*, p. 158.
15. Foxe, *Acts and Monuments*, vol. VI, p. 425; Holinshed's *Chronicle*, vol. IV, p. 23.
16. *The Accession, Coronation and Marriage of Mary Tudor*, trans. and pub. C.V. Malfatti, Barcelona, 1956, p. 72.
17. *Chronicle of Queen Jane*, p. 54.
18. Ibid., pp. 60–1.
19. Holinshed's *Chronicle*, vol. IV, p. 25.
20. Ibid., pp. 24–5.
21. *Original Letters*, vol. II, p. 515.
22. Ibid., vol. I, p. 303.
23. *Cal. State Papers, Foreign, Elizabeth*, vol. L., p. 443.
24. Harleian MS no. 6286; Strickland, *Lives of the Tudor Princesses*, pp. 199 *et seq.*
25. Strickland, *Lives of the Tudor Princesses*, p. 221.
26. Ibid., pp. 229 and 230.
27. Ibid., p. 235.
28. Ibid., pp. 238–24.
29. Conyers Read, *Secretary Cecil*, p. 278.
30. Strickland, *Lives of the Tudor Princesses*, p. 265.
31. *Cal. S.P. Spanish, Elizabeth*, vol. I., p. 468.
32. Strickland, *Lives of the Tudor Princesses*, pp. 277–8.
33. H. Ellis, *Original Letters Illustrative of English History*, 2nd series, vol. II, pp. 288 *et seq.*
34. Strickland, *Lives of the Tudor Princesses*, p. 328.
35. Davey, *The Nine Days Queen*, pp. 335–6.

# SELECT BIBLIOGRAPHY

(Place of publication London unless otherwise stated)

*Acts of the Privy Council*, J.R. Dasent, 32 vols, 1890–1907

Ascham, Roger, *The Scholemaster*, ed. J. Mayor, 1863

*The Babees Book*, ed. Edith Pickert from the texts of F.J. Furnivall, Chatto & Windus, 1908

Beilin, Elaine, *Anne Askew's Self Portrait: Silent But for the Word*, ed. M.P. Hannay, Kent State University Press, Ohio, 1985

Brigden, Susan, *London and the Reformation*, Clarendon Press, Oxford, 1991

*Calendar of State Papers, Foreign, Elizabeth*, 23 vols, ed. Joseph Stevenson et al., 1863–1950

*Calendar of State Papers, Spanish*, 13 vols, ed. G.A. Bergenroth et al., 1862–1954

*Calendar of State Papers, Spanish, Elizabeth*, 4 vols, ed. M.A.S. Hume, 1892–9

*Calendar of State Papers, Venetian*, 11 vols, ed. Rawdon Brown et al., 1864–98

Camden, William, *Annals of Queen Elizabeth*, 1688

Chapman, Hester, *The Last Tudor King*, Cape, 1958

——, *The Sisters of Henry VIII*, Cape, 1960

——, *Lady Jane Grey*, Cape, 1962

*The Chronicle and Political Papers of King Edward VI*, ed. W.K. Jordan, Allen & Unwin, 1966

*The Chronicle of Queen Jane and Two Years of Queen Mary*, ed. J.G. Nichols, Camden Society, no. 48, 1850

Clifford, Henry, *Life of Jane Dormer*, ed. J. Stevenson, 1887

*A Collection of State Papers . . . left by William Cecil, Lord Burghley*, ed. Samuel Haynes, 1740

Curtis, J., *Topographical History of the County of Leicester*, 1831

Davey, Richard, *The Nine Days Queen – Lady Jane Grey and her Times*, Methuen, 1909

*The Diary of Henry Machyn*, ed. J.G. Nichols, Camden Society, no. 42, 1848

Dugdale, William, *Baronage of England*, vol. 1, 1716

# LADY JANE GREY

Ellis, H., *Original Letters Illustrative of English History*, 2nd series, 4 vols, 1827

Elton, G.R., *The Tudor Constitution*, Cambridge University Press, 1972

Foxe, John, *Acts and Monuments*, ed. G. Townsend and S.R. Cattley, 8 vols, 1837

Green, M.A.E., *The Lives of the Princesses of England*, 6 vols, 1855

Gunn, S.J., *Charles Brandon, Duke of Suffolk*, Blackwell, 1988

Hall, Edward, *Chronicle*, ed. C. Whibley, 1904

Harbison, E.H., *Rival Ambassadors at the Court of Queen Mary*, Princeton University Press, 1940

Harleian MS no. 6286

Hayward, Sir John, *The Life and Reign of King Edward VI*, 1630

Hoak, Dale, *Rehabilitating the Duke of Northumberland: The Mid-Tudor Polity*, ed. Jennifer Loach and Robert Tittler, Macmillan, 1980

Holinshed's *Chronicle*, 6 vols, 1808

Howard, George, *Lady Jane Grey and her Times*, 1822

James, Susan E., *The Devotional Writings of Queen Catherine Parr*, Transactions of the Cumberland and Westmorland Antiquarian and Archaeological Society, vol. 82, 1982

——, *Queen Kateryn Parr*, Transactions of the Cumberland and Westmorland Antiquarian and Archaeological Society, vol. 88, 1988

——, *Kateryn Parr – The Making of a Queen*, Ashgate, 1999

Jordan, W.K., *Edward VI: The Young King*, Allen & Unwin, 1968

——, *Edward VI: The Threshold of Power*, Allen & Unwin, 1970

King, John N., *Patronage and Piety: The Influence of Catherine Parr: Silent But for the Word*, ed. M.P. Hannay, Kent State University Press, Ohio, 1985

*Leland's Itinerary – Travels in Tudor England*, ed. John Chandler, Sutton Publishing, 1998

*Letters and Papers, Foreign and Domestic, of the Reign of Henry VIII*, 21 vols, ed. J.S. Brewer et al., 1862–1910

Levin, Carole, *Lady Jane Grey: Protestant Queen and Martyr: Silent But for the Word*, ed. M.P. Hannay, Kent State University Press, Ohio, 1985

*Literary Remains of King Edward VI*, 2 vols, ed. J.G. Nichols, Roxburghe Club, 1857, reprinted facsimile edn New York, 1964

*Literary Remains of Lady Jane Grey, with a Memoir by N.H. Nicolas*, 1825

Loach, Jennifer, *Edward VI*, Yale University Press, New Haven and London, 1999

Loades, David, *Mary Tudor – A Life*, Blackwell, 1989

Madden, Frederick, *The Privy Purse Expenses of the Princess Mary*, 1831

Malfatti, C.V., trans. and ed., *The Accession, Coronation and Marriage of Mary Tudor*, Barcelona, 1956

——, *Two Italian Accounts of Tudor England*, Barcelona, 1953

Mathew, David, *Lady Jane Grey: The Setting of the Reign*, Eyre Methuen, 1972

Mumby, F., *The Girlhood of Queen Elizabeth*, 1909

*Original Letters Relative to the English Reformation (Zurich Letters)*, ed. H. Robinson, Parker Society, 2 vols, 1846–7

Perry, Maria, *Sisters to the King*, Andre Deutsch, 1998

*Polydore Vergil's English History*, ed. Sir Henry Ellis, Camden Society, no. 29, 1844

*Polydore Vergil – The Anglica Historia, 1485–1537*, ed. with a translation by Denis Hay, Camden Society, 3rd Series, no. 74, 1950

Prescott, H.F.M. *Mary Tudor*, rev. edn Eyre & Spottiswoode, 1952

*A Relation . . . . of the Island of England . . . about the Year 1500*, trans. and ed. C.A. Sneyd, Camden Society, no. 37, 1847

Richardson, W.C., *Mary Tudor the White Queen*, Peter Owen, 1970

Salzman, L.F., *England in Tudor Times*, Batsford, 1926

*Sermons of Hugh Latimer*, ed. John Watkins, 2 vols, 1926

*State Trials, Corbett's Complete Collection*, vol. 1, 1809

*Statutes of the Realm*, Record Commission, vol. IV

Stone, J.M., *The History of Mary I, Queen of England*, 1901

Strickland, Agnes, *Elizabeth I*, Everyman edn, 1906

——, *Lives of the Queens of England*, 12 vols, 1840–8

——, *Lives of the Tudor Princesses, including Lady Jane Grey and her Sisters*, 1868

Strype, John, *Ecclesiastical Memorials*, 3 vols, Oxford, 1820–40

——, *Life of John Aylmer*, Oxford, 1821

——, *Annals of the Reformation*, 4 vols, Oxford, 1824

*Syllogue Epistolarum*, ed. T. Hearne, Oxford, 1716

Tittler, R. and Battley, Susan, 'The Local Community and the Crown in 1553: the Accession of Mary Tudor Revisited', Bulletin of the Institute of Historical Research, vol. lvii, 1984

Tytler, P.F., *England under the Reigns of Edward VI and Mary*, 2 vols, 1839

Watson, Foster, *Luis Vives and the Renascence Education of Women*, Edward Arnold, 1912

Wingfield, Robert, *The Vita Mariae Angliae Reginae*, ed. D. MacCulloch, Camden Miscellany 28, Camden 4th series, vol. 29, RHS, 1984

Wriothesley, Charles, *Chronicle of England During the Reigns of the Tudors*, 2 vols, ed. William Douglas Hamilton, Camden Society, no. XI, 1875–7

# INDEX